A Soldier's Life

Raintree | OSPREY
PUBLISHING

Confederate Artillerymen of the Civil War

Philip Katcher • Illustrated by Bill Younghusband

For information, address the publisher:
Raintree, 100 N. LaSalle, Suite 1200, Chicago, IL 60602

First published 2001
Under the title *Warrior 34: Confederate Artilleryman 1861–1865*
By Osprey Publishing Limited, Elms Court, Chapel Way, Botley, Oxford, OX2 9LP
© 2001 Osprey Publishing Limited
All rights reserved.

ISBN 1-4109-0113-0

03 04 05 06 07   10 9 8 7 6 5 4 3 2 1

Library of Congress Cataloging-in-Publication Data

Katcher, Philip R. N.
  [Confederate artilleryman, 1861-65]
  Confederate artillerymen of the Civil War / Philip Katcher.
     v. cm. -- (A soldier's life)
Originally published: Confederate artilleryman, 1861-65. Oxford [England] : Osprey, 2001, in series: Warrior.
Includes bibliographical references and index.
Contents: Enlistment -- Training -- Daily life -- Appearance -- Campaign life -- The artilleryman in battle.
  ISBN 1-4109-0113-0 (lib. bdg.)
  1. Confederate States of America. Army--Artillery--History--Juvenile literature. 2. Soldiers--Confederate States of America--History--Juvenile literature. 3. United States--History--Civil War, 1861-1865--Artillery operations--Juvenile literature. [1. Confederate States of America. Army--Artillery--History. 2. Soldiers--Confederate States of America--History. 3. United States--History--Civil War, 1861-1865--Artillery operations.] I. Title. II. Series.
  E546.6.K38 2003
  973.7'42--dc21
                        2003005279

Author: Philip Katcher
Illustrator: Bill Younghusband
Editor: Nikolai Bogdanovic
Design: Ken Vail Graphic Design, Cambridge, UK
Index by Alan Rutter
Originated by Magnet Harlequin, Uxbridge, UK
Printed in China through World Print Ltd.

CONTENTS

INTRODUCTION

Looking back on his service, Private Val C. Giles, Co. B, 4th Texas Infantry Regiment, recalled, "During the war I used to think the artillerymen were the bravest men on earth. They could pull through deeper mud, ford deeper springs, shoot faster, swear louder, and stand more hard pounding than any other class of men in the service." High praise indeed from a member of one of the hardest fighting Confederate infantry units in the war.

Many of those artillerymen had never seen a cannon before the war. While volunteer militia infantry companies were common in pre-Civil War America, few companies could afford the expense of artillery. Hence, few Americans, save those in the Regular U.S. Army or those who had seen service in the Mexican–American War, had much experience with that arm of service. However, it quickly became obvious that with the amount of infantry organized to take the field, artillery units would have to be organized, manned, armed, trained, and finally, taken into combat.

Anybody who even glanced at the 1860 census data in 1861 must have realized that, given that the Northern states would fight to maintain their country, the South would have no chance of winning its independence. Moreover, the root cause that led Southern political figures to seek independence was slavery, the fundamental principle on which Southern society functioned. Indeed, one South Carolina artilleryman wrote home that "a stand must be made for African slavery or it is forever lost."

However, only a minority of the men who would eventually serve in the Confederate Army had a real stake in slavery as an institution, so the question arises, why did they join? Private Joseph Garey, Hudson's Battery, spoke for many when he wrote, "We are fighting for our inalienable rights & for them we inaugurated the war." Private Robert Stiles of the Richmond Howitzers later wrote that they did not fight for slavery or the right of Virginia to secede, but simply to defend their homes.

There were only three basic types of army units that the volunteers of 1861 could join: infantry, cavalry, and artillery. Of the three, the artillery was the most esoteric. Relatively few rural southerners had seen artillery in action, let alone had any practice on crew-served guns. Therefore,

Volunteers in front of the Charleston Hotel, Charleston, South Carolina, at the very start of the war, December 22, 1860. Many of these early uniformed volunteer companies that entered Confederate service to form the hard core of the South's army were artillery units.

there were basic differences between artillery volunteers and volunteers for other branches of the service.

There were many considerations over which branch of service to choose. Philip Stephenson, Washington Artillery's 5th Company, who had had earlier infantry experience, thought them over when rejoining the army in 1863. "The objection to returning to the infantry service was the extra hardship," he wrote. "If I went back, there were my gun, ammunition, knapsack, and blanket to carry, and there was picket and skirmish duty to perform. All of which the artillery man as a rule escapes. In addition a man in a battery gets many a chance to ride, changing places with drivers who frequently want to walk. On the other hand, the artillery service is thought by some to be the most dangerous, the wounds received likely to be fatal, being caused by shell, solid shot, sharp shooting, etc."

Most artillery units tended to be made up of men from larger cities rather than rural communities. They had the practice in working together and they, more than rural types, would be familiar with artillery and the mechanics involved. Indeed, Confederate artillerymen considered themselves, in the words of Captain Edward Byrne, "the better class of young men." Many came out of colleges, and, indeed, a number of batteries were organized on student campuses. Other batteries had in their ranks machinists, carpenters, tailors, printers, and blacksmiths. One Alabama battery even had as its cannoneers eight doctors, two college professors, the superintendent of education of Tuscaloosa County, and some prominent planters.

"Farmers, mechanics, merchants, laborers, lawyers, university students and theological students, made up the bulk of the company,"

A gathering of South Carolina artillery officers in Sullivan's Island, outside Charleston, in early 1861. Captain A.J. Green, Columbia Flying Artillery, stands left. All wear the prewar South Carolina dark blue officer's uniform, with the man next to Green wearing a field-grade officer's double-breasted coat. (National Archives)

5

wrote Confederate artillery officer William Poague of his new battery. "We thus had the very best material for a battery – men who knew how to manage and take care of the horses and educated, high spirited men for the guns." Successful artillerymen, wrote Robert Stiles, needed four qualities, "intelligence, self-possession, comradeship, loyalty to the gun."

ENLISTMENT

Most of the volunteers simply joined units in which they already had friends and neighbors. Stiles recalled in joining the Richmond Howitzers that the men in it already were "those whom for the most part I met in a social way." Stiles went on to say that, "It was strikingly true that in 1861 the flower of our educated youth gravitated toward the artillery." Stiles' new unit was "made up largely of young business men and clerks of the highest grade and best character from the city of Richmond, but included also a number of country boys, for the most part of excellent families, with a very considerable infusion of college-bred men …" The Howitzers boasted their own glee club, trained by a professional musician, and a "law club" that held mock trials and whose members gave speeches in English, Latin, and Greek.

In the initial enthusiasm of volunteering to defend one's home, many men who otherwise might have waited for commissions joined units as privates. Many of these later regretted the decision. Private Ham Chamberlayne, a lawyer and political leader in Richmond before the war, joined the 21st Virginia Infantry as just such a private in 1861. By February 1862 he was writing home, "I believe I can be of more use as an officer than as a private but I see no way open. A judicial blindness was upon us all, in the beginning of the contest, & 'tis too late for me at least to repair it, by any such means as raising a company …" Chamberlayne managed to get into an artillery battery as a sergeant, with a promise of a commission to follow.

Some units started out life as one thing, only to turn later into an artillery battery. Private J.C. Goolsby, Crenshaw Battery, remembered how his unit formed up as a proposed cavalry company: "On the 14th day of March, 1862, on the Basin bank, in the warehouse of William G. Crenshaw, assembled a number of young men, middle-aged men and boys, all eager to do duty for the State in her defense. Well do I remember the means resorted to by some (at that period none but those

Camp Louisiana in July, 1861, the first camp for the famed Washington Artillery Battalion of Louisiana.

Because of a shortage of actual cannon, many of the fortifications set up by the Confederates around Richmond in 1861 included wooden logs painted black to look like cannon and were actually manned by Southern cannoneers. These were called by both sides "Quaker guns," after the pacifist sect. (Library of Congress)

who had attained the age of eighteen years were eligible) that they might overcome what they in their patriotism believed to be unjust in not permitting them to take up arms and march to the front." In fact, the unit was quickly converted into an artillery company once it reached the army. Company A, 27th Virginia, had already spent time as an infantry company before it was converted to Carpenter's Battery to make up for a lack of trained artillerymen.

As a notice of the skills needed in the artillery, the new artillerymen discovered their pay packets were slightly thicker than those of the infantry. According to a Congressional Act of March 6, 1861: "The monthly pay of the colonel of the corps of artillery shall be $210; of a lieutenant-colonel, $185; of a major, $150, and when serving on ordnance duty, $162; of a captain, $130; of a first lieutenant, $90; of a second lieutenant, $80; and the adjutant shall receive, in addition to his pay as lieutenant, $10 a month. Officers of the artillery serving in the light artillery, or performing ordnance duty, shall receive the same pay as officers of cavalry for the same grade.

"The monthly pay of the officers of the cavalry shall be as follows: of a colonel, $210; of a lieutenant-colonel, $185; a major, $162; a captain, $140; a first lieutenant, $100; a second lieutenant, $90 … The monthly pay of the enlisted men of the Army of the Confederate States shall be as follows … The sergeant-major of cavalry, $421; first sergeants, $20; sergeants, $17; corporals, farriers, and blacksmiths, $13; musicians, $13, and privates, $12 … The non-commissioned officers, artificers, musicians, and privates serving in light batteries, shall receive the same pay as those of cavalry."

Light artillery organization was set up on November 1, 1862, with General Order #81 that called for each four-gun battery to have, "One captain, 1 first lieutenant, 2 second lieutenants, 1 sergeant-major or first

Private John Werth, Richmond Howitzers, a prewar militia unit, wears the letter "H" on his forage cap, indicating his unit was Company H of the 1st Virginia Regiment. He was wounded at the first battle of the war, Big Bethel.

sergeant, 1 quartermaster sergeant, 4 sergeants, 8 corporals, 2 buglers, 1 guidon, 2 artificers, 64 to 125 privates." Heavy artillery units were initially organized the same as infantry companies. On March 3, 1862, Adjutant and Inspector General Samuel Cooper wrote to the Secretary of War, Judah P. Benjamin, that such an organization gave each unit too few officers and NCOs: "Each section of two pieces should be commanded by a lieutenant and each gun should be provided with a sergeant and corporal, so that a company serving a battery of eight guns should have four lieutenants, eight sergeants, and eight corporals; whereas at present organized the company consists of only three lieutenants, five sergeants, and four corporals." Benjamin agreed, sending the suggestion on to Congress, which also agreed, reorganizing heavy artillery to be the same as light artillery batteries on April 3, 1862.

Battery commander Chamberlayne, Crenshaw Battery, explained the organization of a four-gun light battery of 100 men in the field in 1863, stating, "Each gun is drawn by six horses, driven by three drivers postilion fashion & is followed by its caisson or carriage for ammunition with three more drivers, then there are several wagoners for the Battery, a forge driver, two or three mechanics as harness makers, smiths &c, then add for each gun a sergeant, a corporal (a bugler & a flag bearer for the battery), thrown in the chances of 10 percent being always wounded or sick & you find that 25 to a gun does not furnish 10 to 13 actual cannoneers …"

One of the first things done in any new battery was to elect the officers, with every member receiving a vote. Such elections were held well into the final days of the war. On April 23, 1862, Private Garey recorded: "The day was devoted to an election to fill the vacancy made by the recent death of our brave captain, at the bloody field of Shiloh. It resulted in the election of our first lieutenant to that office, who is well worthy to fill that station & we predict that he will in no way lower our opinion in his efficiency & bravery." In cases where officers had proved to be martinets, they lost elections and often resigned their commissions as a result, with a resulting loss of many good officers for the Confederacy.

"This was the usual mode of electing an officer in the army," wrote Joseph Graves, Bedford Light Artillery. "On a given day, the men are ordered to fall in, in the presence of an officer. Then the orderly sergeant calls the roll, and each man as his name is called announces the name of the man of his choice. A teller, previously appointed, hands in his account to the officer, and he announces the result of the election."

"The wisdom of this procedure has been much questioned," wrote William Poague. "Officers who tried to keep up discipline were not popular and failed of reelection. A few were on the other extreme and hence not reelected."

Many of the popular, but inefficient officers were weeded out after an Act of Congress passed November 22, 1862, called for commanding officers of each department to set up an examining board, "… to examine into the cases of such officers as may be brought to their attention for the purpose of determining their qualifications for the discharge of the duties properly appertaining to their several positions."

Indeed, elections arose as a problem for the entire Confederate Army when, in early 1862, as one-year enlistments were coming to an end, Congress passed an act that called for its soldiers to volunteer for service for the rest of the war or be drafted, or conscripted, to that length of term. Volunteers, proud of being such, were dismayed at being labeled conscripts if they refused the new terms. Private Garey noted on May 10, 1862: "Conscript has made his appearance in camp much to the displeasure of our twelve month boys, who made some awful threats against the old gentlemen placid & quiet. We are pressed in for two years more, much against our inclination & wishes; but I suppose we will have to put up with it no matter how much we dislike it. It is very unjust & I fear will cause many to desert the army who would have been free volunteers for the war." "Nothing ever hurt the army any more than the re-enlistment

The regulation uniform for Confederate artilleryman, from a plate in the official uniform regulations book. Some foot artillerymen, who manned siege guns around city defenses, actually managed to obtain copies of these uniforms, but the average Confederate artilleryman wore a short single-breasted jacket.

of the men, and the election of new officers," summed up Bedford Light Artilleryman Graves.

Once a unit had been formed and its officers elected, its strength had to be maintained in the face of losses to disease, wounds, and men changing units. Individual batteries sent officers and NCOs back to their home bases constantly during the war to open recruiting stations, stay awhile, and bring back new men. Captain Charles Squires, Washington Artillery, had such duty in January, 1863. "Sergeant M.R. McGoughy and myself were detailed to proceed to Jackson, Miss. and there to establish head-quarters for recruits ... At Summit, Mississippi, I secured several recruits. Some New Orleans friends were located at this point. [After several weeks,] Time's up! Back to old Virginia!" The captain and sergeant then accompanied their recruits back to Lee's army.

Moreover, civilians aged between 18 and 45 could also be conscripted, unless in one of the exempted job categories such as newspaper editor, cleric, state official, or overseer on a plantation with a set number of slaves.

TRAINING

There were two ways in which men were trained for the artillery. The first was as a group, usually at some open area near their home or, having gotten to a military camp, in the camp of instruction where they were first organized into a battery. The second was a more informal way, as new recruits or conscripts joined the unit and received individual training from an NCO. Most new recruits came directly to the unit from civilian life, while conscripts generally reported to a state or regional camp of instruction where they received basic military training before being sent on to a unit.

Private Goolsby recalled his unit formed, "with about eighty men and boys, as we marched to Camp Lee, all in bright uniforms, to commence the actual duties of the soldier." Camp Lee was the artillery camp of instruction nearest Richmond, one of many scattered throughout the South. Captain John C. Shields, 1st Howitzers, was sent to organize Camp Lee on a farm in late 1861. Having obtained a copy of the 1860 U.S. Army artillery manual, he had used that book to teach tactics and drill to the 75 batteries that passed through his camp between November, 1861, and June, 1862. For battalion drill, practiced when he had enough batteries together for such, he used a translated French manual.

Indeed, obtaining manuals for training would be a major problem for the fledgling Confederate artillery. Virginia Military Institute tactics instructor William Gilham published a widely used manual before the war, one often reprinted in the South, that had a section on light artillery tactics. It was, however, not universally used. Lieutenant-colonel Snowden Andrews, who commanded a field artillery battalion, recalled that the only manual available at first was an old U.S. Army manual which referred to "horse artillery" in which every member is mounted rather than field artillery, in which only a handful are mounted. Hence, Andrews recalled, "the explanations of the various maneuvers were found to be complex and confusing." In fact, Andrews did not get a good field manual until he found on the battlefield at Mechanicsville

A British-made artillery button bearing the Roman letter A, along with a British-made general service button, marked C.S.A, that would have been used for all branches of the service. The A button was the regulation type of button required, but general service and even captured Union and Confederate infantry buttons were sewn on uniforms issued to many artillerymen. (Author's collection)

ABOVE **An original jacket from the Army of Tennessee bearing the regulation artilleryman's buttons with a Roman A. (John Lyle)**

ABOVE CENTER **The side of the Lyle jacket.**

ABOVE RIGHT **The back of the Lyle jacket.**

"a little work on Field Artillery, by Mr. Patten, late officer United States army, published in New York, in November, 1861." Eventually Andrews went on to publish his own Confederate manual.

According to Andrews' manual, training new recruits was to be "given by the non-commissioned officers, under the supervision of the chiefs of sections.

"The instructor should never require a movement to be performed until it is exactly explained and executed by himself. It should be left to the recruit to take the positions and execute the movements directed, and he should be touched only to rectify mistakes arising from want of intelligence.

"Each movement should be perfectly understood before passing to another. After they have been properly executed in the order laid down, the instructor no longer confines himself to that order.

"The instructor allows the men to rest at intervals during drill, and for this purpose he commands *Rest*. At this command the recruit is no longer required to preserve immobility. At the command *Attention*, the man takes his position, and remains motionless."

Andrews also explained what training should be given new artillerymen: "The preliminary instructions to be given to *artillery recruits* is the same as that given to the *infantry soldier*, previous to his instruction in the manual of arms, embracing *the position of the soldier, the facings, and marching* … Besides this, *artillery recruits* are early instructed in the *saber exercise* … In addition to the foregoing, the light artillery soldier should be taught how to mount a horse, and practiced at riding, in order that he may be fitted for duties of driver, and any other position requiring a knowledge of horsemanship. He should, moreover, be instructed in the care of horses, and in the manner of harnessing and hitching them."

Heavy artillerymen, those who manned the giant siege and seacoast guns, were not sent to artillery camps of instructions, but instead were

trained on the actual guns they would serve. Recalled Colonel J.G. Pressley, Wee Nee Volunteers, of his unit's arrival in the Charleston, South Carolina, defenses in April, 1861: "We went into camp near the 'Star of the West Battery.' I had the use of the guns of that battery for the purposes of instruction, and rapidly taught the men the heavy artillery drill. I was aided by Major P.F. Stevens, then Superintendent of the Citadel Academy. The company took to this new drill with great alacrity, and it was not long before they became as proficient in artillery as they were in infantry tactics."

Learning all this meant many hours on the drill field. "We drilled all day in the sleet," wrote Billy Vaught, 5th Company, Washington, "but I enjoyed it. We drill 8 hours a day, rain or shine. I enjoy it all. Aint I a queer fish."

All this drill paid off. According to a notice in the order book of the 5th Company, Washington Artillery, in the spring of 1863: "By recent tests our Battery can be gotten ready to move to any point in 15 minutes. Yesterday Batt. hitched up in 14 min; piece #6 hitched up in 4 min. Today batt. hitched up in 9 min (piece #6 in 7 min.) Allowing from 5–6 minutes for storing of personal effects of cannoneers 6 min; hitching up 9 min [gave a total of] 15 min."

Higher commands sometimes recognized excellence in drill. Captain James Douglas, Douglas' Texas Battery, wrote home in April, 1863: "On the 4th of May there will be a prize drill of the batteries in our [Polk's] Corps. The best drilled battery will have awarded to it a beautiful banner. My boys think if they have a fair showing they will take the prize – all hands agree that the contest will be between my battery and Scott's. If we take the prize, we will then be required to drill against the best drilled battery in Hardee's Corps."

Drill sometimes included live firing at targets, although, given the cost per round, this was not greatly encouraged. "We are going out target shooting this evening with our battery, which promises some rare sport," Private Garey recorded in October, 1861. "As we have not had the opportunity of trying them on the Yankees, we expect to try them at any rate to find out how we can shoot, though we are noways anxious to know the result as we are pretty good marksmen having tried them once before at short range." In fact, the next day Garey had to admit they were not such good marksmen. "Our boys were a little mistaken in their marksmanship yesterday, their shots not being as good as they anticipated but ranging rather wildly for a first class gunner. The distance was four hundred yards; the mark about eight feet square & the closest shot being about eighteen inches from the mark."

Both live rounds and the more common blank rounds still presented dangers to new artillerymen. Private James Lunsford, Douglas' Texas Battery, described a practice gone bad in his first days of drill: "At one time, while executing the maneuvers of the battery drill of flying artillery over the rough prairie, the powder in an ammunition chest became ignited and all three chests of a caisson were blown up. Fortunately there was no other damage done. Some of the horses were badly scared, and as it was a new experience to the boys, we were more or less excited."

Drill was, of course, used both to teach the men to handle their weapons and to get them used to military life. It was for recruits, both at a camp of instruction or seacoast fort, the hardest thing simply to get used to unaccustomed military discipline. This was always a problem in the Confederate army, and the artillery, even with a better class of recruit, proved no different. Recruits tended to be either from better-off families who were more used to slaves taking their commands

Men of the 5th Company, Washington Artillery, in one of their first camps. They wear their prewar dark-blue uniforms with scarlet-topped caps. The elaborate camp equipage, including wooden tent floors, would not last long. (Library of Congress)

Another group of the 5th Company, Washington Artillery, prior to Shiloh. The standing man is a corporal. (Library of Congress)

than to being commanded themselves, or rural, independent types who believed that nobody was their superior and they would take no orders from anybody. Officers, who had to maintain discipline, fought this problem, without a great deal of success, throughout the war.

Dismayed at his first taste of discipline, one "'high private in the rear rank' actually wrote and sent in to the captain an elegant note resigning his 'position'," recalled Robert Stiles of the Richmond Howitzers, a unit made up of a large number of First Families of Virginia scions. William Poague, then a battery commander, found that, on taking command of the Rockbridge Artillery, he had to arrest several men for desertion. "They became greatly incensed at me as if I had initiated the disciplinary action and as if I ought to or could have prevented it. One of them, a member of a prominent family, became so offensive and insulting that it was with the greatest difficulty that I controlled my temper and prevented a personal altercation, which I thought he wanted to bring on." Poague realized that with Southern volunteers, an officer had to win them over first, and then be able to discipline them. "After a while these things ceased to worry as I became more and more assured of the respect and confidence of a large majority of the men," he wrote.

Poague was a volunteer like his cannoneers, but officers who had been in the U.S. Army didn't understand they had to win their soldiers' respect and confidence first. They tried to initiate regular army discipline. Private James Lunsford, Douglas' Texas Battery, recalled one such attempt: "We had guard lines around the quarters and sentries walked their beats in silence except the 'Who goes there?' If any one approached; and in the night to call out the 'All is well!' every hour. We submitted to all this cheerfully and thought we were soldiers; but when a severe North Arkansas winter came upon us we demanded fire at the guard posts. Major Brandfute, who had spent twenty years in the regular army, remonstrated with us, appealed to our patriotism and the oath we had taken. He was replied to by Dick Small, W.S. Waites and others, to the effect that he, himself, had taken oath, and that if his oath as an officer meant anything he should protect the health of the men under him and not sacrifice their lives in such weather, in the interest of discipline, when there was not an enemy within 200 miles. The fires were extinguished by a detail sent out by Major Bradfute from another company, but the Texans, rallying to the sentinels from camp immediately rebuilt them. Major Bradfute reluctantly submitted, and remained afterward our friend."

Punishment in the light artillery often included being strapped to the spare wheel mounted on the back of a caisson in a spread-eagle position. Joseph Graves mentioned one man in his battery who took a watermelon "as much out of fun as anything else" out of the wagon of a civilian selling them but was then caught. He "was strapped to a caisson. Our officers did not allow any one to steal, even to satisfy their hunger."

DAILY LIFE

Once recruited, the battery gathered at a camp of instruction or army post where it began some drill while waiting to receive its horses and guns.

Private Sam Thompson, Douglas' Texas Battery, wrote home to describe his typical day as a new soldier on September 20, 1861: "At daybreak, 'Reveille,' at which I am compelled (reluctantly) to arise from my bed of blankets, and go forth from my comfortable tent; 'Roll Call.' Then 'Stable Call,' at 7 o'clock; 'Breakfast Call.' After which the Bugle sounds Second Stable Call and the drivers turn their horses upon the beautiful prairies around us; at 8$\frac{1}{2}$ o'clock the cannoneers drill at their pieces – a beautiful and interesting exercise. An hour for drill, and all return to camps to pass the time as they choose; some reading, others writing – by far the greater number engage in some game, ball, base, pitching dollars, marbles, cards, chess, are all in vogue here.

"At 4 p.m. the Battery turns out for drill, as do all the Regiments camped here, when the scene is quite animating.

"Drums, fifes, bugles, banners, plumes, glistening bayonets and sabers – long lines of infantry here and dense columns of horsemen there – while the artillery-men wheel and dash with their heavy guns, from point to point as if at play. This over, to camp, supper, and 'Tattoo' ends the day. Such is camp life, after all not miserable and devoid of pleasure."

Even after turning in, life in camp continued a routine. Private Samuel Thomas, Douglas' Texas Battery, wrote home of the scene: "The sentinels call their posts in regular garrison style every half hour. At 10 o'clock, the cry is heard away up in the north side of the quarters, Post No. 1, 'Ten o'clock and a-l-l's well.' The cry is taken up and we hear Post No. 2, '10 o'clock and a-l-l's well.' Thus Post No. 3, '10 o'clock and a-l-l's well,' and sentinel after sentinel cries his post until the entire line have responded, thus breaking the silence of the night every half hour by the musician voices of our sentinels, seems to disturb the monotony of guard duty during the night season, while it serves as a solace to the

The first page of the light artillery manual produced in the South in 1863 to meet training needs.

ANDREWS'

MOUNTED ARTILLERY DRILL;

COMPILED

ACCORDING TO THE LATEST REGULATIONS

FROM

STANDARD MILITARY AUTHORITY,

BY

R. SNOWDEN ANDREWS,

LIEUTENANT-COLONEL COMMANDING BATTALION ARTILLERY.

CHARLESTON:
EVANS AND COGSWELL.
1863.

15

Artillerymen wait while their dinner cooks in the large pot over the fire behind them. A caisson can be seen in the distance.

sleeping garrison, as it reminds them of the vigilance of those who watch while others sleep."

Battery commander Chamberlayne described his routine in camp in early 1863: "I rise & attend the reveillee roll call at 6 A.M. to see to the drivers attending to their horses for an hour, breakfast about 8; send up the sick to the surgeon at 8; drill from $11\frac{1}{2}$ to $\frac{1}{2}$ P.M. have the horses again groomed and watered & fed from 4 to 5, retreat roll call at 6, dine at 5, Tattoo roll call at 8; go to bed at pleasure."

Sundays were largely free of military routines. Private Garey was one of those who was delighted to see Sunday come. "Once more I welcome the day of rest, as I seldom welcomed it before I became a soldier. None know but those who have tried it, how tiresome it is to be constantly under restraint; the constant tramp; the same pound of duties, & the petulancy of officers, is enough to worry a martyr."

Sundays often brought visitors, including local ladies, and most of them were attracted more to the guns than anywhere else in camp. Samuel Thompson wrote home in January, 1861: "The artillery is the drawing card with the fair sex. The ladies visit us and inspect the big guns and give the soldier boys the benefit of their smiles almost every day." In the same way, Private Garey noted that September in Missouri: "We have had a great many visitors of the fair sex come to gratify their curiosity as to how a military camp looks & how they manage to get along. They are very curious to know how we manage to shoot these large guns & always go off well satisfied with the prowess & superiority of the Southern boys over the Yankees, at the same time expressing their warmest wishes to our welfare."

This was, for most of the men, the first experience of living in tents in the field. Many grew sick and died in these early camps, often with childhood diseases such as measles, to which few Confederate soldiers had been exposed before, taking a surprising toll. "The Measles are still claiming more attention," Private Garey noted in his diary in October, 1861, "several more have been added to the lists."

These first camps were generally more generously furnished with tents and equipage than would ever after be the case. John Morton wrote of his experience as a new first lieutenant in Porter's Tennessee Battery in early 1861: "At that time the company was well supplied with cots and blankets, and this was the only period of the war when this condition came within the author's experience." These often were quite cozy. Second Lieutenant Robert Walker, Jeff Davis Artillery, described his first winter camp to his sister: "We have a fire place to one of our tents, which we use as a sitting room the other we keep for a bed room. The Capt. has a tent to himself. All the men have fire places to their tents or houses; and we get on very well in that particular." The horses didn't make out as well. "For the horses we have brush sheds, but they do little or no good."

Later in the war tents became rare, but when men went into quarters for any length of time they made log huts for themselves. Ham Chamberlayne, outside Petersburg, wrote in December, 1864: "My Camp is a model, tho' I say it; regularly laid off in streets & dwelling houses made of the ever useful Virginia pine, kept scrupulously, regularly, neat and all things done decently & in military order – My own quarters & those of my officers are comfortable enough for anything, roomy, clean, warm & with excellent beds, frame bedsteads, foundation made of slabs such as are wonted when singles cannot be used for lack [of] nails [which were not produced in any number in the South during the war], on these is laid plentiful quantity of pine tags & the grand result is a close imitation of a French hair mattress."

A rabbit makes the mistake of entering a camp full of hungry Confederates. Rations like this that were not issued made up an important part of the average artilleryman's daily diet.

This drawing by a veteran of Confederate artillery service shows entertainment in the camp. The instrument is the uniquely American banjo.

Other camps were more informal. The camp of the Washington Artillery in 1862/63 saw each mess, or group of friends who shared their rations, "thrown upon its own resources and ingenuity to make themselves as comfortable as they can," Adjutant William Owen wrote. "Some dig a deep square hole or cellar, with a fireplace and chimney at one end. Over the hole is stretched a tent 'fly,' and then, by covering the floor with clean straw, a comfortable dwelling-place is made. Others are in Sibley tents, with large mud fireplaces and chimneys; and, as wood is plenty, all hands are enjoying a much-needed rest. Head-quarters are in tents, and the whole camp is in a large pine woods."

As for his own quarters at Petersburg in 1864, Owen described them as containing "a camp-table, a wooden inkstand from Harper's Ferry, one old camp-stool. A small valise contained a change of under-clothing, and a leather haversack, that was always carried on my saddle, held all my toilet apparatus, – looking-glass, comb, brushes, soap, and towel. My blankets were the red artillery blankets of the 'Feds,' and my large India-rubber cloth, which was rolled about them, when travelling, was a souvenir of 'Chickamauga.' My pistol and saber hung on a peg on the rear tent-pole. The saber was *presented* to me by a Federal officer captured at Drewry's Bluff."

Many of the officers and men brought slaves from home to take care of their cooking, washing, and the like. John Morton even brought three "negroes who cooked for his mess and looked out for his comfort," he later wrote. He was hardly alone in such luxury. Ham Chamberlayne wrote home in October, 1862: "John still remains, a model camp servant. I find that he can both cook & wash well enough. He is absolutely content."

According to Adjutant Owen in 1861, "When the command left New Orleans for Virginia every mess had its two or three servants, or 'boys,' as they were universally called. These 'boys' would take charge of the mess, and, in very many cases, were the slaves of the officers and men. They were expected to black the horses, forage for provisions at times, rub down private horses, etc. Many were accomplished body-servants, good barbers, and the like. Quite a number served faithfully until the end of the war; some deserted to the enemy when it was bruited amongst them that the war had set them free, and appeared in the Northern papers as 'intelligent contrabands.' "

African-Americans with the army also often entertained their masters. Philip Stephenson recalled when in camp near Mobile, Alabama, "Good cooking, banjo strumming, and dancing 'break downs' now became the order of the day. We used to pit the African-Americans against one another in the clog dance, and there was one 'boy,' as black as charcoal …but a good hearted simple soul, Tony Barrow's boy Charles. He would get on the floor and with cheers and compliments and 'taffy' keep shuffling his huge feet until he would nearly drop."

Often soldiers with a number of slaves rotated those at the front with those at home, taking advantage of their trips back and forth to send letters and pay back and have food and clothing brought up to the camp. This continued throughout the war, although as the war went on and rations became harder to get the total number of blacks in any given battery became smaller. "Tell Agatha if Fred dont kiss her on sight," wrote Ham Chamberlayne, then a battery commander outside Petersburg, on sending his servant home, "in spite of smiling whites & grinning blacks I will hold him no true man but a recreant knight unworthy of her favors."

Of course, many such slaves took advantage of their situation to escape to Union lines and freedom. A slave belonging to an officer of the Jeff Davis Artillery, who had fled during the 1862 Maryland campaign, was captured as a Union officer's servant, at Chancellorsville. He was sent back, well guarded, to Alabama.

Even so, there was quite a number of African Americans serving through to the end as cooks and servants for all ranks, not just officers. Private Dick Shirley, a member of William Poague's artillery battalion, actually threw a Christmas dinner in the trenches around Petersburg for his battalion commander, some battery commanders, and some visitors from the Navy. "The menu consisted in part of oysters, fish, roast turkey, various vegetable, corn bread-a-la-Tuckhoe, and tropical fruits and the inevitable Christmas eggnog." Poague noted that Shirley's "cook, George, was perhaps the best in the army." Moreover, George "was a great forager."

Even with servants available, soldiers often had to try to keep their clothes as clean as possible themselves. Robert Stiles recalled "that one of the most difficult things for a soldier to do is keep his person and his scant clothing reasonably clean, and that one of the large memories of my soldier life is a record of 'divers washing.' " This was a new

A Confederate artillery veteran drew this engraving of a snowball fight in a Confederate winter camp. The novelty of snow to so many inhabitants of the Deep South led to a great deal more excitement about the weather in Confederate camps than in Union camps.

A group of Confederates drawn by the sight of a Northern photographer aiming his camera across the Rappahannock River at Fredericksburg in 1862 after the battle there. Notice the nondescript appearance of the troops. The man standing in the frock coat appears to be an officer. (National Archives)

experience for most men who, even if they didn't own slaves, left things like washing to the women or the laundries at home.

Other new experiences included learning new games of chance and visiting establishments in nearby towns which would have shocked the folks back home. Indeed, many soldiers, especially those of a religious bent – the majority of soldiers – expressed dismay at how army life had turned their comrades. James Douglas wrote home in December, 1862: "Sallie, I have not learned to drink and swear like nearly everybody else in the army but have become a constant companion of the pipe, what do you think of that? I have not resorted to this disagreeable practice for the purpose of drowning my sorrows so much as from a love of the weed, perhaps I will quit it when the war closes." Private Garey noted on Christmas, 1861, "Today is Christmas & with the exception of three or four, every man is drunk in the company & trying [to see] how bad they can act." Indeed, Garey wrote again next March that, "Men live in camp as if they cared neither for the present or the time to come. The Devil almost holds his sway supreme & sin is almost a necessity with the majority."

Drinking, for the majority of light artillerymen at least, who were away from civilian population centers, was not a serious problem in the army. "For good reason," Washington Artillery's Stephenson noted, "not that we were more virtuous, but because liquor was harder to get at the front... We had no money, for pay days became rarer and rarer, and if we had, there was no liquor to buy."

Although the majority of Confederate artillerymen came from homes in which religion was important, it was relatively rare that they got to attend services while in the service. Infantry regiments were authorized chaplains, but artillery batteries, which also tended to serve independently, were not. The Baptists, believing in a strong separation of church and state, sent colporteurs to travel with the army and hold services when possible, rather than assign regular chaplains. Thus they were able to reach artillery batteries more readily than other sects did. Private Garey noted in his diary on May 26, 1862: "Nothing new or uncommon has occurred in camp since yesterday, except that we attended the preaching of a sermon on yesterday, which is quite a rarity for our company; though from the attendance it appeared that they were in no way anxious to encourage continuance of divine service but cared but little about it."

Chaplains were, however, authorized at the battalion level, and when all the separate batteries came together in a camp as a battalion, they often had regular services. William Poague, commanding a battalion in the winter of 1863/64, recalled: "Our Presbyterian chaplain, Reverend James M. Wharey, had services on Sundays and prayer meeting once during the week. Reverend Hugh Scott, of the Episcopal Church, visited camp preaching a number of times and holding communion. All of us except some of the Baptists attending the communion services. We had a visit and preaching also by Dr. J.B. Jeter, a noted Baptist minister from Richmond. A large number of the men were professing Christians; many of them highly intelligent and educated gentlemen; and not a few earnest and devoted followers of Christ." The Episcopal dioceses of Virginia and Georgia also created special army and navy versions of the period *Book of Common Prayer*, which they distributed to soldiers and sailors.

Revivals swept through the various Confederate armies from time to time. A long period in winter camps, especially when near towns where civilian churches and preachers were available, usually marked a revival time. Robert Stiles, whose father was a Presbyterian minister, described

In winter camps, the two sides took advantage of lulls in fighting to trade, Southern tobacco for Northern imported coffee, which was impossible to get in the South due to the naval blockade of its coasts.

A period sketch of cannoneers holding their position, having built a shelter against the sun on a hot day.

a typical meeting during a revival time in the winter of 1862/63: "Long before the hour appointed the men would begin to gather, intent on getting into the church and securing a seat. Thereafter every moment was occupied with some act of worship of uncommon intensity and power. The singing, in which everyone joined, was hearty and impressive; the prayers, offered generally by the men themselves, were soul-moving 'cries unto God;' the preacher was sometimes a distinguished divine from Richmond, sometimes one of the army chaplains, sometimes a private from the ranks, but whoever he might be, he preached the gospel and the gospel only."

Adjutant William Owen, by then a major in the Washington Artillery, recorded in January, 1865, in his diary from Petersburg: "The men have built a chapel just behind my tent, and have prayer-meetings nightly. The whole army has taken to praying, and if prayers accomplish anything we should whip this fight yet."

However, it should be said that the overall religious tenor of the Confederate army is often overemphasized. Joseph Graves, who later became a minister himself, noted after the war that, "The members of the Jordan battery were men of high moral character but not religious. Among the men of the Battery no hymns were sung and no prayers meetings were commenced and continued … An exemplary minister of the gospel on a visit to their camp offered to preach for a given amount; they declined the offer, not wishing to make merchandise of the gospel."

Reading was very popular when possible. Captain James Douglas wrote home from Ft. Kennesaw, near Marietta, Georgia, June, 1864: "I am passing the time better than you would suppose since we are disagreeably situated. I read a portion of my time, attend to my duties another portion, and sleep a very liberal portion. I have finished Scott's poetry and read some other books. Read Scott. You will fall in love with Ellen Douglas of *The Lady of the Lake* and Lucy of *The Bridal of Triermain*… I am reading Shakespeare now." Later, July, 1864, "I am reading *Macaria* or *Altars of Sacrifice* by the author of *Beulah*, Miss Evans of Mobile. It is an interesting little novel."

Reading material was generally scarce, however. Philip Stephenson recalled in the winter of 1863/64, "So rare were books, that I remember the only volumes I read in camp for a year or more. One of Miss Muhlbaack's novels, *The Court of the Emperor Joseph*, I think, and Hugo's *Jean Val Jean* – grimy, backless, with pages off at both ends. But I read what I could – and guessed at the rest." Victor Hugo's novel *Les Miserables* appeared while the war was going on, and an edition published in Richmond sold very well. Army of Northern Virginia cannoneers began to refer to themselves as "Lee's Miserables."

In much the same way, letter writing was highly popular, but difficulties with the Confederate post office, especially after the Mississippi River was captured making mail to the West sporadic, put a damper on regular mail. Often soldiers took advantage of furloughed soldiers or returning servants to bring their mail to nearby homes. Receiving letters was also the highlight of a soldier's day. John Walters, Norfolk Light Artillery Blues, noted after Gettysburg that a local letter carrier had arrived. "He has brought a large number of letters for our boys, but none for me. This nearly filled up the measure of my misery. I wonder if I am forgotten."

Some soldiers kept diaries. Stephenson, however, believed that, "Diaries were rare. I remember only one man that kept a diary… Suitable books could hardly be had, we had no money, and the life we led made such impracticable."

Not all rural Southerners, whose state governments largely discouraged public education, could read or write. Some soldiers took advantage of their military service to make up for that deficiency. Battery commander Chamberlayne, in the lines around Petersburg, wrote that his battery officers started "a school $1\frac{1}{2}$ hours a day for the men of this Company nearly one half of whom are ignorant of reading or writing. To read, to write (I shall not teach in this department) and a little ciphering [mathematics] will be our highest ambition. You know I am no advocate for education, specially for the masses, but there are many boys in the Company, some of them very bright and it seems my duty to do all I can for them."

Since Confederates usually spent their winters in friendly territory, camp life in winter quarters, when near civilians, could be pleasant. Samuel Thompson wrote in January, 1861: "Occasionally the officers get up a dance in their quarters and not infrequently the boys get out and attend the country dance." Even in 1864, when Forrest's artillery was camped near Columbus,

Infantrymen from the 4th South Carolina help build fortifications for the artillery, directed by engineer officers. (Frank Leslie's Illustrated News)

Mississippi, John Morton recalled that, "The ladies were unwearying in their efforts to relieve the tedium of camp life. The most delicious dinners, the most comfortable clothing, and the rarest of entertainment were provided with a lavishness that could not be surpassed. Sometimes there were as many as three parties in a single night, and frequently all-night parties were turned into all-day picnics the following day."

Even late in the war, officers pulled themselves away from the front to get into Petersburg or Richmond. "We had 'delightful starvation parties, the men furnishing the music and the hostess the bread and butter," Owen wrote of 1864. "The girls are always prettily dressed, and they don't care if you know what a hard time they have to do it. They say they twist and turn all their old things because they can't get new ones. Fashion plates are scarce." Enlisted men who got into such towns were equally ragged, so it was typical for the lucky visitor to town to borrow clothes from his comrades, a clean shirt from one, a tie from another, a good pair of boots from a third, and a nice hat from a fourth.

Quite possibly because so many Confederates came from the Deep South, where snow was rare, most winters found the men engage in large-scale snowball fights. Philip Stephenson noticed on the first snowfall: "Our Louisiana boys were shivering and demoralized. They were not used to snow, and that was the biggest one most of them had ever seen!" They soon adjusted, however. Robert Stiles recalled in the Army of Northern Virginia in the winter of 1862/63, "Entire brigades lined up against each other for the fight. And not the masses of men only, but the organized military bodies – the line and field officers, the bands and the banners, the generals and their staffs, mounted as for genuine battle. There was the formal demand for the surrender of the camp, and the refusal, the charge, and the repulse; the front, the flank, the rear attack. And there was intense earnestness in the struggle – sometimes limbs were broken and eyes, at least temporarily, put out, and the camp equipment of the vanquished was regarded as fair booty to the victors."

Some bored and ill-paid soldiers turned to theft, sometimes in good humor and sometimes less so. Soldiers often targeted each other. Private Garey noted in January, 1862: "There is some little perplexity in our company as to the means of finding out the perpetrator of several thefts in our camp. Three navy repeaters [0.36 caliber revolvers] have been stole at different periods without leaving any trace by which to track the thief. They were stolen [out of] the tents." More often, however, they picked on nearby civilians.

Northern civilians and soldiers alike were always astonished at the number of African-Americans seen in Confederate camps. Officers and even quite a few privates kept their personal servants with them at the front throughout the war. Often they wore cast-off Confederate uniforms, leading outsiders to believe incorrectly that they were attached formally to the army, often in a fighting capacity.

Stonewall Jackson's men forage captured Union supplies at Manassas Junction during the Second Bull Run campaign. The Union Army was a major supplier to the Confederate forces.

Private Thompson wrote that in January, 1861: "Speaking of apples, yesterday a mountain farmer was just outside the guard lines selling a load of very fine pippins. The boys formed a conspiracy against him – five or six of them took sacks and all pressed up to buy, and every man filled up his sack and handed it back to his partner, who returned to the camp with the apples. Each handed out a $20 bill to be changed. Having no change, the rustic became confused. Each man held on to his bill but demanded change, which could not be had. While this was proceeding the lynch-pin was removed from the wagon. The farmer finding that his business was not prospering concluded to move on – doing so, as he drove off down the hill, his wagon fell to pieces and his fine apples rolled in all directions. The men came to his relief by filling their pockets and shirt bosoms as they assisted him in restoring matters to a proper shape."

Many of these escapades were done as much as a lark as theft. Private Thompson admitted a general sense of humor found among Confederate artillerymen, something not found to the same degree in the opposing army, in February, 1861: "Camp life is monotonous and time drags heavily. Now and then we get up a breeze by playing practical jokes upon each other, and occasionally a citizen is the victim." Even senior officers were not immune to this form of humor. On April 1,

1862, Private Garey recorded that, "Gen. Bowen loves a joke about as well as any other man, especially when he can make it convenient to play off one as he did this morning to the amusement of the knowing ones on his staff. He issued an order early this morning for the marking with Indian ink on the left shoulder every man in our company & allowing but twenty-four hours for the completion of the job. The ink & instruments were sent for with all due gravity & dispatch in order to finish the work in good time. Meantime there arose considerable discussion upon the subject concerning the meaning of such orders & the propriety of submitting to the operation. How it would have ended is hard to say but the discussions were ended by the appearance of another dispatch stating that this was the first of April & the Pettus Artillery were badly fooled."

In the long days of winter, most soldiers' minds turned to getting home. Furloughs were granted to many of them, especially in the period in 1862 when the government tried to get soldiers enlisted for one year to volunteer for the duration of the war. Garey noted in his diary in January, 1862: "The furlough fever has taken hold upon our company to alarming extent which threatens those not taken with in with double duty during their abscense [sic]. Some twelve or fourteen have given their names as Volunteers for two years more under the new provision of congress which give [sic] sixty days furlogh [sic] to those joining for that length of time or the war."

Although morale among Confederate artillerymen seems unusually high, compared to other branches of service, there were times that the call of home was stronger than the pull of duty, and men, unable to get furloughs, did desert. At first, when such men where captured, they were put through a ceremony similar to that reported by Garey in December, 1861: "We were called upon yesterday to witness a scene not often witnessed in our army Viz. the whipping & drumming out of the service of four deserters in sight of the whole division consisting of six regiments & a battalion of infantry, one battalion of Cavalry & two light batteries in all about seven thousand men. The Army was drawn up in a hollow square two ranks deep commanding a view of the whole Division by every individual. In the center guarded by a Company of Infantry, a detachment of twelve men acting as executioners of the orders & one company of drummers, stood the four prisoners with shaved heads; three of whom were tied to a stack of arms, hand & foot and received fifty lashes with a rawhide upon the naked back, after which they were marched around the entire line, hat in hand & drummed outside. Then we returned home." In later years, shooting deserters would be more common than whipping them.

In many cases, however, deserters found themselves beyond the reach of Confederate authorities. Colonel John Haskell, an artillery battalion commander, recalled two heroic cannoneers who had received sick leave. "Going home, they found their cabins and their families as they had left them, with fish a-plenty and a better market – the United States soldiers – than they had known. They took the oath of allegiance and stayed at home. Their families needed them. There was no glory for them, no cross of a legion of honor. Their duty to a cause they scarce understood, hardship, suffering, and danger of death were all they had to return to. The danger and suffering to them and their families were great, their reward invisible. Who can wonder that they stayed home or judge them harshly? I for one cannot. The true wonder is that any held out."

Whenever possible, troops got copies of newspapers both to read and later to trade with the enemy for coffee and other items unavailable in the South. Dealers from Richmond and other cities near military camps would bring out the newspapers for sale. A contemporary drawing by Edwin Forbes.

APPEARANCE

The men received their first uniforms on joining their units. Units that had been organized prior to joining the Confederate Army usually arrived in their militia uniforms. Artillerymen usually wore the traditional blue with red trim. Joseph Graves described the initial Bedford Light Artillery uniform, which was typical of most, as being "made of a dark blue material, the coat buttoning straight up in front, fastened by the waist by a belt, with a short skirt below it. The pants and coat are trimmed with red, which is the style for artillery suits, and above all, is a cap to match, mounted with two brass cannon crossed obliquely."

Officially, the Confederate artillery uniform consisted of a red copy of the French kepi, trimmed with gold braid for officers, with a double-breasted grey coat with red collar and cuffs, and sky blue trousers with red stripes for officers and non-commissioned officers. Artillery staff officer Francis Dawson described his first uniform as "a gray tunic with scarlet cuffs and scarlet collar; an Austrian knot of gold braid on each arm; two bars of gold lace, denoting the rank, on each side of the standing collar; gray trousers with broad red stripes; a scarlet kepi, trimmed with gold braid, and commonly known, by the way, as the 'woodpecker cap.' "

In fact, the Confederate government could not afford such an elaborate first issue, even if it could find material and makers to produce all it needed. As a result, "Each member furnished his own uniform and equipment, officers their own horses," recalled a member of the prewar militia battalion, the Washington Artillery of New Orleans. This prewar volunteer battalion was clad in blue when it arrived in Virginia and took to the field in the First Manassas with red flannel strips tied around the left arm above the shoulder as a field sign. Members of the battalion's

A guncrew of the Palmetto Light Artillery. This unit was in the defenses of Charleston, so they remained reasonably well fed and equipped. Still, the variety of uniforms worn by the different members gives an idea of the appearance of the mid-war Confederate artillerymen. (Library of Congress)

fifth company at Shiloh turned their blue jackets inside out in action. All exchanged them for grey jackets as quickly as possible.

Still, it was typical for the average Confederate artilleryman to receive his uniforms from home rather than from the government. In October, 1861, Joseph Garey reported that "we received a uniform this morning from the citizens of Panola Co. & also a goodly number of blankets & under clothes from the same kind of donators. We may now be said to be able to stand the winter's storm of this region, or a cooler one, for which we expect to fight before long."

Many early uniforms included fanciful touches, but these were soon abandoned, not only due to rough weather and exposure, but also to the constant comments of fellow Confederate soldiers. First Lieutenant John Morton, at Fort Donaldson in early 1862, recalled how he, in his "handsome artillery uniform, with a black hat, one side turned up and a feather in it, was a striking figure. One of the Confederates, rising from the trenches, upon seeing him cried out : 'Pretty bird, I'll catch him a worm in the morning.' Lieutenant Morton, realizing the situation, took out the feather and rolled it in the dirt."

Private S.C. Williams, 13th North Carolina Light Artillery, which was formed in December, 1863, and served in the Army of Tennessee, in a typically informal light artilleryman's uniform.

Individual soldiers were largely supplied from home through the first two winters of the war, but the central government was able to take over supplying uniforms thereafter. These uniforms were made in quartermaster depots in various places in the country, and all switched waist length, single-breasted jackets for double-breasted frock coats. The seven-button jackets made in Richmond through 1862 had red trim on the cuffs, around the collars, and on the shoulder tabs; thereafter they were made of plain gray jeans cloth or wool. These were mostly worn in the Army of Northern Virginia. Six-button jackets made in Georgia had red jampot cuffs and collars, although inspectors complained that artillerymen rarely drew these branch-of-service jackets, receiving instead jackets with medium-blue infantry collars and cuffs. These mostly appeared in the Army of Tennessee, although some were issued to the Army of Northern Virginia, too. Similar jackets were made in the Deep South, but with only branch-of-service wool collars and plain cuffs. Many depots issued plain jackets as well. All were to have brass buttons bearing the letter A on them. In 1864, dark-gray wool jackets with red trim on their shoulder tabs began arriving from an Irish maker, Peter Tait. Copies of the French kepi, with red bands and gray sides and tops, were made in southern depots, although wide-brimmed slouch hats were the preferred headgear.

As military dress was rarely issued as an entire uniform, but in bits and pieces, there was a distinct lack of uniformity among artillerymen. Edward Moore, Rockbridge Artillery, described himself in the summer of

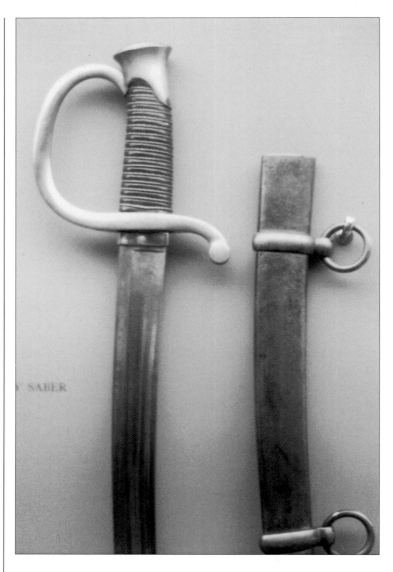

Y SABER

Officially, every light artilleryman was to carry a light artillery saber, such as this prewar Northern-made model. In fact, few bothered to, and even those issued them tended to leave them behind for ordnance officers to pick up and reissue to the cavalry. (Smithsonian Institution)

1862 as wearing, besides a "tall, drab-colored fur [hat] of conical shape, with several rows of holes punched around the crown for ventilation," a "lead-colored knit jacket … adorned with a blue stripe near the edges, buttoned close at the throat, and came down well over the hips, fitting after the manner of a shirt. My trousers, issued by the Confederate Quartermaster Department, were fashioned in North Carolina, of a reddish-brown or brick-dust color, part wool and part cotton, elaborate in dimensions about the hips and seat, but tapering and small at the feet… This is an accurate description of our apparel. Among our fellow-soldiers it attracted no special attention, as there were many others equally as striking."

Officers had to supply their own uniforms. They, too, preferred the short jacket for field use, marked with their rank badges, which were one, two, and three bars for lieutenants and captains, and one, two, and three stars for majors and colonels. Many officers had the Austrian knot in gold or red on each cuff, the number of braids indicating rank, too. Lieutenants had one braid; captains, two; and field-grade officers, three. The same number of braids were worn on the red kepi with its black band.

Although they were to wear double-breasted frock coats both for dress and when in heavy artillery, generally the waist-length jacket was more popular in the field. In October, 1862, Ham Chamberlayne wrote home: "About a coat I am not at all anxious, don't be in a hurry about it. The Jacket I think will fit me as it is, merely have a pair of bars on each side of the collar, and an edging of gold braid to the cord on the sleeve. The jacket is exactly what I want. Please have two pockets inserted in it." By 1864, officers, whose pay did not keep track with inflation, were allowed to receive cloth from the Quartermaster Department to have made into uniforms. Many managed to get the same depot jackets their enlisted men drew.

Non-commissioned officer grade was marked by red chevrons worn, points down, on both sleeves. Although some men could not get red lace for such stripes, apparently many managed to do so through to the end of the war. General Lee, near a Napoleon then in disuse during the battle of Spotsylvania, spotted a corporal of the Jeff Davis Artillery and, "seeing my stripes, asked me if I was a gunner, and answering him in the affirmative, told me to take charge of it, which I did." Indeed, artillerymen always tried to have their uniforms trimmed red. As late as the spring of 1865 Charles Squires, by then a major commanding an artillery battalion in Texas, described his "command in their new uniforms trimmed with red …"

After long marches and hard campaigning, quartermaster officials were often behind in re-equipping the men, who began to look quite ragged. Joseph Graves described such a time during the Knoxville Campaign: "Especially there was a lack of shoes. I have read a letter, in which comrade Thomas W. Reed is spoken of as walking about the camp in Russellville with his feet tied up in rags …"

Equipment brought by the average soldier in 1861 included, in many cases, a camp chest with cooking and dining equipment. Wrote Robert Stiles: "The wagon train of the First Company, Richmond Howitzers, during the first nine months of the war was, I verily believe, quite as large as that of any infantry brigade in the army during the grand campaign of '64. Many of the private soldiers of the company had their trunks with them, and I remember part of the contents of one of them consisted of a dozen face and small number of foot or bath towels …" Later, Stiles himself never even bothered to carry a plate, knife or fork, even when a battalion adjutant, eating instead from a tin cup or frying pan by 1864.

The government initially issued swords to every man in each battery, along with the necessary sword belt. The heavy artillery sword was a copy of the U.S. Army M1832 foot-artillery sword which had an all-brass hilt molded in a scalloped decoration, looking like eagle feathers, straight cross quillons, and a straight blade 19 inches long. The scabbard was leather mounted with brass. Although these swords were a total waste of time, they were still produced by a number of Southern makers including The Confederate States Armory, Wilmington, North Carolina, and E.J. Johnston & Co., Macon, Georgia, which produced 150 of them

Artillerymen liked to get revolvers for their personal defense whenever possible. Officers and sergeants were often issued revolvers, such as this Southern-made copy of the Colt 0.36 caliber "Navy" revolver. Unlike the all-iron-framed Colt, this revolver has a brass frame because of the lack of iron in the South. (Russ Pritchard collection)

A battery arrives on the battlefield through mud, with the infantry battle line seen to the extreme left. Only the drivers rode, while the cannoneers ran or marched beside the guns and limbers.

for the Choctaw Artillery. Additionally, a number of makers, whose names are unknown today, produced variations of these swords, some with the letters CS on the quillions and others quite plain.

Light artillerymen carried a copy of the U.S. Army M1840 light artillery saber which had a curved blade 32 inches long, a wood grip covered in leather with a twisted brass wire around it, a single brass knuckle-bow ending in a Phrygian-helmet-pattern pommel. Scabbards were iron, although many Southern-made copies used brass for the scabbards. Copies of these swords were made by Louis Haiman & Brother, Columbus, Georgia; Hayden & Whilden, Charleston, South Carolina; William J. McElroy & Co., Macon, Georgia; Thomas, Griswold & Co., New Orleans, Louisiana; and James Conning, Mobile, Alabama, under contract from the State of Alabama; as well as a variety of makers whose names are unknown today.

"The artillerymen, who started out with heavy sabers hanging to their belts, stuck them up in the mud as they marched, and left them for the ordnance officers to pick up and turn over to the cavalry," Richmond Howitzers Private Carlton McCarthy recalled. William Owen wrote, "How we have reduced our equipment since active service began! Knapsacks have been voted a bore, and have been or will be thrown aside. On leaving home each man had his revolver for 'close quarters,' and the saber was part of the regulation uniform. Both are in disgrace. The revolver will be traded off, sold, or sent home, and the sabers (all that are left, for many have disappeared during the past week) will be turned over to the cavalry.

"Even the officers will hereafter strap theirs to their saddles, or, better still, hang them up in the company wagons.

"A blanket snugly rolled inside of a rubber cloth, the ends tied together and thrown over one shoulder, will hold all the necessary

Corporal, 3d Company, Richmond Howitzers, with issue equipment
(see plate commentary for details)

6

5

3

2a

12
FRICTION PRIMERS.
C.S.Laboratory.
RICHMOND ARSENAL.
No. 186 4

2

1

4

WRy. 00

A

B

Rockbridge Artillery on the march

WRJ.01

The Crenshaw Battery moves up a piece by hand

C

A Confederate gun crew attempts to remove a 12-pounder Napoleon by prolongue

D

The Louisiana Guard Artillery defends Kelly's Ford

F Allegheny Artillery firing (see plate commentary for details)

WRY. 01

Seacoast fort guns (see plate commentary for details)

G

Quarters in the field

WBY. 01

H

A battalion winter headquarters

The personal items of an artilleryman

9

4 **Tobacco**

6

8

5

7

3

1

1a

2

11

10

J

WRY. 00

change of clothing; the haversack will carry the crackers and bacon, the comb, the soap, and the towel, and the tooth-brush will decorate the button-hole of the jacket, together with the tobacco-bag."

Willy Dame of the Richmond Howitzers described the men of his battery in campaign trim, in which "each man had one blanket, one small haversack, one change of underclothes, a canteen, cup and plate of tin, a knife and fork, and the clothes in which he stood. When ready to march, the blanket, rolled lengthwise, the ends brought together and strapped, hung from the left shoulder across the right arm; the haversack – furnished with towel, soap, comb, knife and fork in various pockets, a change of underclothes in the main division, and whatever rations we happened to have in the other – hung on the left hip; the canteen, cup and plate, tied together, hung on the right; toothbrush, at will, stuck in two buttonholes of jacket or in haversack; tobacco bag hung to a breast button, pipe in pocket." Leaving behind revolvers and swords, artillerymen didn't need leather belts, either, and discarded them as well. Officers didn't carry much more. Battery commander Chamberlayne wrote in April, 1863, that he did not bring "anything beyond an extra pair of pants and two suits of underclothing, all in the hand trunk [carpet bag]; and my great coat."

Indeed, covered with dust or mud from riding or walking with the guns the usual Confederate cannoneer appeared uniformly filthy in a relatively short time in the field. Many individuals have told how General Robert E. Lee once saw his son Private Robert Lee of the Rockbridge Artillery, and was unable to recognize the battle-weary soldier as his young son.

CAMPAIGN LIFE

Spring eventually rolled around, and with it, the artillerymen would break up their winter camps and head back on the campaign trail. Adjutant Owen described the scene: "Instantly comes the order for 'Boots and Saddles,' and the welcome notes from the bugle are given tongue. The boys yell with delight; the quiet bivouac is changed as if by a magician's touch; all is hurrying to and fro. But few moments pass, and the Colonel's loud-voiced order comes: 'Tention! Drivers, prepare to mount. Mount!' 'Cannoneers, mount!' 'Column, forwa-r-r-rd!' And the Battalion moves out into the road towards the battlefield."

These were men who traveled light. Tents were rare in the field, most cannoneers simply rolling up in their blankets under the guns or limbers in the evening after caring for their horses and feeding themselves. One Jeff Davis recalled in fall, 1862, that in his camp, "although a wall tent or Sibley [tent] graces an occasional locality, the most of the men ensconce themselves in bush built shelters of various shapes, in fence corners, under gun-blankets, eked out by cedar boughs, or burrow semi-subteraneously [sic] like the Esquimaux." There, after learning to ignore the lice that constantly bore into their skin, the men would fall asleep until the bugle call that woke them the next morning.

The same humor seen in camp was also seen on a march. Wrote Owen: "Any peculiarity of costume or surrounding of any person was sure to bring out some remark that would set whole regiments in a roar." Even high-ranking officers were not immune; one Virginia colonel was noted for wearing a high-topped hat and carrying a blue cotton umbrella. "Come out of that umbrel; I see your legs!" shouts would

Artillerymen often went into battle facing enemy artillery fire, as in this wartime sketch.

A gunner sights his piece in action, in this drawing by a veteran of the Washington Artillery.

come from the ranks as he rode by. "Come out of that hat; I want it to boil my beans in!"

The men also entertained themselves by singing. "The men were in fine spirits," wrote Philip Stephenson, of a march during the Atlanta campaign. "They were nearly always so, those 5th Co, W[ashington] A[rtillery] men! We were singing. I remember 'Annie Laurie,' 'En-pi-dee' (great favorite with us), 'Anne Darling,' etc."

Often, especially when getting close to the battlefield, guns, limbers, and caissons had to pass through trails not made for them. John Walters recalled one such time when "twice the order was given for the cannoneers to go to the front with axes, to cut a road through the woods, the main road being perfectly impassable."

Such work made them all pretty dirty, pretty quickly. Some men attempted to remain lice-free, difficult as that was. William Poague recalled how in February, 1862, he had his "first and last fight with 'gray backs' (vermin). I went to a creek on a cold windy day, took off my new flannel underwear, sunk it with rocks in the cold water, washed myself clean, put on new flannels intending to return in a day or two to get my shirt and drawers – minus the little creatures as I hoped; but an order to hitch up and move at once left me no time to look after them and I saw them no more."

Keeping clean on the march was always a problem. Artillerymen had some advantages over the infantry, though. Philip Stephenson recalled: "Our washings were confined as a rule to the face and scant at that, the water being brought in and poured out of our canteens. Sometimes a wash basin was in evidence, sometimes a bucket. We of the artillery, were compelled to always have *one* bucket (the leather or heavy rubber one belonging to the piece, and used for swabbing out the gun during an engagement), so, sometimes that was utilized. One of our greatest inconveniences was in regards to our *teeth*. How to keep them clean … Tooth brushes were plentiful enough, for they were made with twigs, generally of the gun tree, one end being split into a sort of brush."

Early on, rations were plentiful. Joseph Graves described their first rations for one day as, "$1\frac{1}{2}$ pounds of flour, $\frac{1}{2}$ pounds of bacon or beef, some sugar and coffee, some peas, beans or rice, and some salt." Confederate commissary officials were unable to maintain these rations, and food was often scarce on campaign. Private Linn Tanner, Boone's Louisiana Battery, recalled how hungry they all were during the siege of Baton Rouge: "About twenty days prior to the surrender of Boone's Battery a company of one hundred and twenty-five men in charge of six brass field pieces was reduced to the small allowance of three ears of corn each daily [sic]. Small rations truly when it is known that this corn was raised in the pine hills, where fertilizer was not abundant, and the corn had never attained to the size of full-grown ears, but had stopped perforce somewhere between childhood and the adult stage and earned the name justly of 'pinewoods nubbins.' It was really a most laughable sight to see the men at 'ration time,' which, in a spirit of humor, was announced by the commissary sergeant getting up on the wagon and calling out in a loud voice, 'Pig-gee, pig-gee, pig-goo-ah!' with a long-drawn accentuation on the last syllable. On hearing the call every man in the command would fall on his all-fours and begin squalling and grunting in all the various tones and chords known as 'hogainity;' and on reaching the wagon and receiving the corn, which was pitched to the recipient, he would place one ear in his mouth and with one in each hand make his return to quarters, playing as many pranks as possible to keep up the jollity of the camp."

Some campaigns were more notable for hunger pangs than others. J.C. Goolsby felt that the campaign in Virginia in 1864 was the worst time for that. He wrote that that time was, "one of great privations on the part of the Confederate soldiers, whose rations at this time were not sufficient in quantity or very elegant in quality – namely, corn meal of almost all colors, with Nassau pork, which was indeed the most unpalatable meat that one ever ate, with occasionally a few peas – red peas. And then

Moving a gun forward into action by hand, the limbers having been sent to safety in the rear.

Artillerymen from General Floyd's Confederate forces in western Virginia in 1861 prepare to shell a Union camp in this period sketch.

the condition of those peas – well, I will not attempt to describe it. Think of cooking three days' rations of this yellow meal and carrying it in your haversack with the pork, and you can imagine our condition. The meal would of course become sour, and the meat – well, it would soon be running out of the haversack, for mind you, this was in the months of July and August."

Even in winter camps the food was rarely better. Edwin Mussina of the Washington Artillery in the Army of Tennessee recalled in the winter of 1863/64: "The Bill of Fare of all the Army could be written in two words Bacon and Meal. Corn Bread and bacon for breakfast. Bacon and Corn Bread for dinner and as for supper a very small cup of mush and corn coffee without sweetening." Coffee, a drink as necessary as water for many Americans, was sorely missed, as it had to be imported and the blockade made that impossible. "There was no effort made to provide sugar and coffee for the soldiers," Joseph Graves noted, "if they were on hand, they would be issued in small quantities; but if not on hand, the soldiers went without them."

The result was that men foraged for additional food as far and wide as they could. At Petersburg, the men had the time to hunt for food in the local area. During the winter, Goolsby wrote: "Time and again have I known the men to go down to the ponds and break a hole in the ice and fish, staying sometimes all night on its banks, only to be rewarded by the catching of a catfish, which would occasion great joy among their messmates. I don't know what the men would have done had it not been for that very delightful fruit, which seemed to flourish in this section of the country – the Dinwiddie persimmon." In the lines of Petersburg, John Walters noted one day: "Today I ate my initiatory dish of Pussley, a weed that grows about here in great abundance. For camp use, I find it an excellent substitute for the greens which we eat at home … as we Confederate soldiers have learned to eat almost any and everything, I do not see why we should not pitch in to Pussley with our characteristic vim, especially as many of us have many inches of hide which sadly needs filling out …"

Other hunting tended to be done in farmyards under cover of darkness. In October, 1862, Lieutenant Chamberlayne wrote home that "Squirrels, hares & partridges fall an easy prey & here an 'old red' [hen] succumbed." A month later he wrote that he had "been fortunate in foraging, getting at various odd times & places sometimes butter, sometimes honey, eggs, milk, or cabbages …"

An 1861 mortar battery on Morris Island facing Fort Sumter before the bloodshed began. These volunteer gunners are still in civilian attire.

Lack of food meant vitamin deficiencies that showed themselves in various ways. Robert Stiles noted that, "perhaps the most peculiar and striking fact or feature of the physical condition of General Lee's army during the latter half of the war was night blindness – the men affected being unable to see after sunset, or a little later... The doctor tells us that these symptoms were to be accounted for as among the expressions of an anemic and scorbutic condition, which itself resulted from lack of proper and sufficient nutrition."

Cooking was also difficult on campaign. Recalled Private Tanner: "There being no way to grind this corn into grist, the Confederate soldier adopted such means as were at hand to utilize it. Some boiled it, some beat it into coarse meal by using an ax head, and others roasted it in the ashes."

Cooking utensils, so well packed in the cases that accompanied the volunteers of 1861, were quickly abandoned. Private John Purifoy, Jeff Davis Artillery, later wrote: "Every old Confederate soldier remembers the split Yankee [tin] canteen, each half of which could be readily turned into a helpful convenience. A frying pan, a stewpan, and a corn and roasting ear grater are a few of the useful implements into which they were usually transformed... The same old soldier has seen the bark slipped from certain trees in the early spring, and the sections divided equally, each of which made an excellent substitute for a bread tray."

Men foraged for other things besides food. Clothes, especially things like boots and hats which were always in demand, were sought in civilian stores. On their way into Maryland in 1862 a group of the Washington

Artillery came across a small store that had a number of old-fashioned bell-crowned beaver hats with long naps on them, something 20 years out of style. One man tossed away his ratty old cap and put one of these on, resulting in everyone having to have one. These elite Louisiana cannoneers fought the Battle of Antietam in such odd headgear.

Dogs accompanied a number of artillery batteries on their line of march. The Troup Artillery of Virginia, for example, took care of a dog the size of a small raccoon which took up residence with the battery when it was in West Virginia. Battery members named him Robert Lee. The dog of the Richmond Howitzers, known as Stonewall Jackson, was a white Welsh fice with some black spots. These dogs were generally known for taking a place in the battery front when in action, barking at the enemy. When a battery had to change position under fire, some cannoneer would scoop the dog up and drop it into a partly empty limber chest. Number 6 would let him out when the battery was in its new position.

The most important animal to light artillery on campaign was the horse. Confederate horses, like their masters, were often short on forage. Moreover, the constant employment exhausted them before their time. John Walters noted on the retreat from Gettysburg that his battery suffered because of the "breaking down of our horses which have not been sufficiently fed for the last three weeks. In fact, you see horses lying by the side of the road dying from exhaustion and literal starvation. Our company, though losing no guns, has lost some twelve or sixteen horses …"

Artillerymen were always looking for new horses. During invasions of the North, horses were relatively plentiful, and artillerymen took advantage of impressing all they could find. Private Goolsby recalled of the Gettysburg campaign: "A party was made up headed by Lieutenant

A crew of the Washington Artillery Battalion in action at Fredericksburg. The gunner aims as No. 5 brings up the next shot in his hands rather than the regulation haversack.

John Hampden Chamberlayne of our battery, with Sergeants Smith, Newman and Mallory, besides several others of the battalion, and started out in the mountains to purchase horses. The party soon came upon the picket-post of the Jessie Scouts, of the Federal army, when Ham Chamberlayne picked out about half a dozen of the men who were armed with revolvers, put himself at the head of them and led a charge. The picket-guard fell back on the regiment, and the whole party were captured and sent to prison."

THE ARTILLERYMAN IN BATTLE

Men going into battle prepared themselves in various ways. Some prayed, others joked, some went through their belongings to make sure nothing that would embarrass them would be found in case of the worst happening. John Morton pulled out a handkerchief from his pocket to stop potential bleeding when wounded in one action, only to have a deck of cards fly to the winds. Until then he'd not played cards, and had picked this deck from a looted depot. Seeing them fall, he "looked upon the gay pasteboards and thought what his mother's feelings would have been killed with such things in his pockets, [and] he registered a vow never to gamble …" Edward Moore knew a battle was upon his battery when he saw "the invariable profusion of playing-cards along the road," adding that "cards were always thrown away by soldiers going into battle."

When waiting in line of battle, especially when placed in exposed positions for a long period of time while not firing a shot, stress could be exhausting, especially for new troops. Robert Stiles recalled a situation when his side was facing the Army of the Potomac in the early stages of the Peninsular Campaign, in which "one of our detachments

Confederate artillery retreating through Mechanicsville under enemy fire. (Frank Leslie's Illustrated News)

broke down utterly from nervous tension and lack of rest. I went in as one of the relief party to bring them out and take their places. It was, of course, after nightfall, and some of these poor lads were sobbing in their broken sleep, like a crying child just before it sinks to rest. It was really pathetic. The men actually had to be supported to the ambulances sent down to bring them away."

The first time actually going towards certain combat proved a terrifying experience. Private George Jones, Stanford's Mississippi Battery, heading towards Shiloh, noted in his diary: "I have the shakes badly. Well, I am not alone – in fact, we all look like shaking Quakers. Scared? Oh, no, only the old-fashioned rigor. We have several bowlegged in line, and you ought to see their knees knocking together."

Quickly enough, however, the word would arrive at the battery to move forward. At that point the battery would march onto the field in column, then go into line. Stiles recorded this part of battle during the Peninsular Campaign: "Once across we were ordered, 'Forward into battery, left oblique, march!' which elaborate movement was executed by the men as if on drill. I could not refrain from glancing around, and was amazed to see every piece, limber, caisson, and man in the exact mathematical position in which each belonged, and every man seemed to have struck the very attitude required by the drill-book. And there we all stood, raked by a terrible fire, to which we could not reply, being really a second line, the first – consisting of infantry alone – having passed into the dense, forbidding forest in front, feeling for the enemy."

Artillery largely fought at fairly short ranges, since the concept of indirect fire was unknown and sighting was done directly along the bore. They might fire against enemy batteries at 2,000 yards and infantry at 500 yards. Moreover, much of the land fought over was in woods and brush where ranges were further reduced. Therefore, Union fire would

Confederate heavy artillerymen on Drewery's Bluff, overlooking the James River below Richmond, shell Union ironclads with their large Columbiads.

51

begin cutting down cannoneers even as they were going into position. Edwin Moore went into combat the first time as "a shell hit the off-wheel horse of my gun and burst. The horse was torn to pieces, and the pieces thrown in every direction. The saddle-horse was also horribly mangled, the driver's leg was cut off, as was also the foot of a man who was walking alongside. Both men died that night. A white horse working in the lead looked more like a bay after the catastrophe."

Eventually the battery would be in position, and the order would go out to spread out in battery front, to engage the enemy. Once the battery was in line of battle, the limbers and caissons took their places in the rear. By the manual, there was to be only six yards between the butt of the handspike and the nose of the lead horse, but this was a sure horse killer. "After Gettysburg it was our habit", wrote Stiles, "when a piece became engaged, to send the horses to the rear, to some place of safety, preferring to run the risk of losing a gun occasionally rather than the team that pulled it." Indeed, horses were so valuable that in the 1864 campaign in northern Virginia, Stiles reported that when artillery officers met the first thing they asked each other was, "How many horses did you lose?"

The first target of any battery was usually an enemy battery. These counter-battery fights were usually tough affairs, and indeed, most gun-crew casualties were caused by artillery fire rather than musketry. Private Jones's battery went into battle at Shiloh: "We were ordered to silence a battery of nine pieces that had our range, just in our front. Before we could fire a gun a shell blew up one of our ammunition chests; another cut off the splinter bar of the third detachment; another almost cut our wheel rider (Bowen) in two. He was killed instantly. Wm. Jones had his right arm shot off. Oh, how I wish that I were a dwarf instead of a six footer … [Still,] we opened with our six guns and an awful artillery duel was kept up for some minutes (seemed like an hour to me). Finally we succeeded in silencing the battery … With our well directed fire we disabled every piece save one."

Once actually in a fight, an artillery gun crew was simply too busy to have time to think of anything but keeping the gun working. "It takes ten cannoneers (exclusive of drivers) to make a gun detachment," Robert Stiles wrote. "Each man his special part to perform but all indispensable to the perfect working of the piece, so that each man is dependent upon all the rest."

Each cannoneer was referred to by a number that described his part in the operations, save for the gunner and the chief of the piece. Philip Stephenson described each soldier's functions: " 'No. 1' rammed and sponged out the gun when foul, the sponge staff having a rammer at one end and sponge at the other. 'No. 2' loaded, or put the charge in, standing at the left of the muzzle. 'No. 3' stood behind 'No. 2' at the reinforce of the piece with his thumb (a little pad on it) on the touch hole while the loading was going on. 'No. 4' stood behind 'No. 1' and opposite 'No. 3,' put in the friction primer and pulled the lanyard. 'No. 5' was at the trail and moved it from right to left as the corporal, who always sighted the gun, directed. He had a hand spike for this purpose. 'Nos. 6, 7, and 8' carried the ammunition from the limber chest to the gun, and when the limber chest was out, from the caisson. The limber chest was always a regulation distance behind the gun, and the caisson still further back at regulation distance. That is, if possible. And under shelter if possible."

Men spent hours on the drill field practicing this elaborate dance. Battle is where all that drilling paid off. Men gave of themselves freely, even thoughtlessly, for the good of the team. Stiles was serving a

The garrison of Fort Sumter under Union naval bombardment. The guns on top of the fort's walls can't even be brought into use because of the enemy fire. (Frank Leslie's Illustrated News)

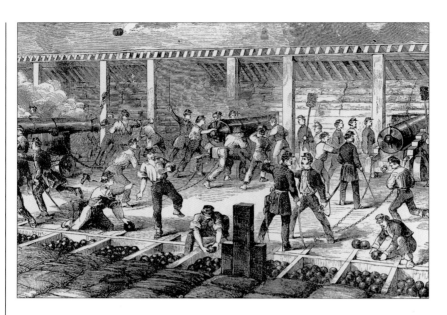

Cannoneers on a floating, protected battery fire on Fort Sumter at the beginning of the war.

gun during the Peninsula Campaign when he saw, "No. 3 [the individual who kept his leather thumb-stall on the vent during ramming] stoop, clapping his right hand upon his leg below the knee, and then I saw him topple slowly forward, never, however, lifting his thumb from the vent, but pressing it down close and hard – his elbow strained upward as his body sank forward and downward. The heroic fellow had been first shot in the calf of the right leg, and as he bent to feel that wound a bullet crashed through his skull; but his last effort was to save No. 1 from the loss of his hands by premature explosion as he rammed home the next charge."

A battery under infantry and artillery fire was a hot place indeed. Adjutant Owen described one gun in action at Fredericksburg: "Corporal Ruggles, who, with sleeves rolled up, has been ramming his gun, suddenly throws up his hands and falls backwards with a ball in his spine. Perry seizes the sponge-staff as it falls from Ruggles's hands, and takes his place. The sharp ring of a bullet, striking the face of the piece, is heard, and Perry's arm, having been shot through, drops helpless at his side; he has been severely wounded. Rodd is holding vent; his elbow-joint is shot away. Everett steps into his place; a bullet strikes him and he falls. As he is laid in a corner of the work with Ruggles, he said, 'Let me do something boys; let me cut fuses.' "

Often, fighting at close quarters, the men did not stand as in the drill manual. Once, during fighting around Atlanta, Washington Artilleryman Stephenson remembered that, "Will Tutt, who rammed and sponged, and I, who loaded, found it certain death to stand up. So we crouched by the muzzle of our gun on either side, loading it in that position." In such heated action, despite dangers from premature explosions, sometimes other niceties of drill were also ignored. At Chickamauga, for example, John Morton noticed one of his cannoneers in action: "Jimmy Woods, acting No. 5, was bringing cartridges from the caissons and limbers to the guns. Captain Morton noticed that he had them in armful lots and reprimanded him. 'Jimmy,' he said, 'don't pile the cartridges at the guns that way. A spark from a friction primer or piece might cause a serious explosion. Just bring two – give one to No. 2 and hold the other until the gun is fired, and then return for more.' "

Indeed, most gun crews exposed their ammunition so they could set fuses and get it to the gun faster. This could often be dangerous. John Haskell recalled once a cannoneer "was sitting with his comrades in a gun-pit, where a quantity of fused ammunition with some loose straw thrown carelessly on it lay around them. The straw caught fire from a bursting enemy shell. Cartridges and shells began to explode, and it looked as though all might be killed, when the man … quickly picked up shell after shell, some of them with their fuses burning, and dropped one after the other into a small mud-puddle nearby. When practically all were in, one of them burst in his hands, but wonderful to say only taking two of his fingers."

Such dangerous practices were even more common at Petersburg, where exposing one's self during a run between gun and limber to the deadly aim of Union sharpshooters caused cannoneers to act unsafely. Recalled J.C. Goolsby: "The section to which I was attached was placed up on a parapet with just sufficient space to work the two guns, and not space enough to work them advantageously or with safety, as we came near losing the No. 1 at our gun, owing to the nearness of the guns to each other, our No. 1 stepping in to sponge, as he thought the gun had been fired (the smoke from the other causing him to be misled), which was not the case, the No. 4 at that time being in the act of pulling the lanyard, and he would certainly have done so had not the No. 3, who was then a small boy, and who had remained upon the parapet when the gun was fired (not being able to get up and down in time), stepped over the trail of the gun and caught hold of the lanyard.

"After remaining here about twenty-four hours the enemy opened upon us with their heavy guns, they having calculated the distance with accuracy, and soon dismounted one of our pieces and exploded several rounds of ammunition, which the men had accumulated near the guns to prevent having to run to the limber-chest under fire every time the

A Confederate gun emplacement along the Atlantic coast that has been attacked by Union fire, the heavy siege gun having been blown off its carriage and thrown into the side. One can only imagine what would have happened to any gun crew working this particular cannon when the Union shell hit. (Library of Congress)

guns were fired. This was done in violation of positive orders to the contrary, but the men paid dearly for it, as two of them – Hardgrove and Coleman – lost their lives. The sufferings of these two men were terrible, and the explosion of the shells caused all of us to lie very low, which called forth loud cheering from the enemy, who could see the effect of their shots."

While cannoneers at the front had their firing drill to keep their minds occupied, those who held horses in the rear had no such luck. William Poague, at Fredericksburg, went to the front when his guns opened fire. "As I passed driver John Conner holding his lead horses by a strap, flat on his breast and head up against a sapling, I said: 'Hello, John, that's a mighty small protection for your head.' He replied: 'Yes, Captain, but if there was a ground squirrel's hole near by I think I could get into it.' I had it from one of our men who is good authority that a certain fellow was stretched out behind a good sized stump with his nose within twelve inches of a pile of filth, when another seeing the situation and coveting that stump for himself exclaimed, 'Look at that stuff near your face.' 'Pshaw, go away! it smells sweet as a rose,' he replied, and still stuck to his stump."

Artillery was often called to move in battle. At Murfreesboro in December, 1864, Philip Stephenson recalled: "The aim of the opposing battery was very accurate and our officer kept us changing positions to break it." Usually in such a case, the guns would be reattached to the limbers and pulled away by horses. However, the cannoneers themselves could also move their guns. J.C. Goolsby recalled at the Second Manassas: "But suddenly we hear the words, 'Cannoneers, mount! Forward; unlimber! Fire by prolong!' And right here let me say that this was the only occasion in which this character of firing was ever practiced by our battery."

The guns made obvious targets, and not only the men but the guns paid the price. After Cold Harbor the bronze Napoleons of the Richmond Howitzers, wrote Robert Stiles, "looked as if they had smallpox, from the striking and splaying of leaden balls against them. Even the narrow lips of the pieces, about their muzzles, were indented

OPPOSITE **Saying goodbye to a wounded comrade being removed from the battlefield by ambulance. During the battles near Richmond, civilians of the Richmond Ambulance Committee took many Confederate wounded from nearby battlefields to hospitals in the city.**

in this way. One of the guns, I think of Manly's battery, was actually cut down by musketry fire, every spoke of both wheels being cut."

If enemy infantry or cavalry actually penetrated the battery area, the men were largely unable to fight them off, having abandoned pistols and sabers long before getting into battle. Captain Joseph Chalaron, 5th Company, Washington Artillery, had his battery overrun by Union cavalry outside Atlanta in 1864. As the saber-swinging Yanks broke into the area, Chalaron yelled to one of his cannoneers, "They're on us! Have you a weapon?" The answer came back, "Not a penknife!" In much the same way, Charles Squires' Washington Artillery battery was overrun

at Chancellorsville. "With a wild yell one regiment broke through our lines on the left, drew up facing us and about a hundred yards in our rear, cutting off all chance of escape. I waved my handkerchief and called out to them not to fire on us."

Other times, of course, the artillery, supported by infantry prevailed, and the attacks were turned back. Either way, eventually the battle was over. The men were exhausted, drained. Edward Moore, after the Second Manassas, "felt myself exhausted and faint from over-exertion in the hot sun. Remembering that my brother David had brought along a canteen of vinegar, gotten in the big capture of stores a few days before, and thinking a swallow of it would revive me, I went to him and asked to get it for me. Before I was done speaking, the world seemed to make a sudden revolution and turn black as I collapsed with it."

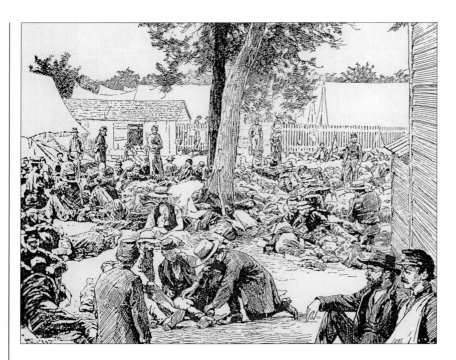

A field hospital after a battle, such as this one at Savage's Station after the Battle of Gaines' Mill, was a terrible place to be. Overwhelmed surgeons couldn't keep up with the flow of wounded, leaving many to wait unattended on the fields around the hospitals.

Many men, after it was all over, discovered that battle was an experience they wouldn't have missed for anything. William Poague first saw combat at the First Manassas, where he saw, "Johnston and Beauregard with their staffs, pass in a sweeping gallop; a terrific roar of cannon and musketry is heard in front; wounded and stragglers come creeping along to the rear, dodging into the fence corners to avoid our battery in its headlong rush. The smoke of the battle rises above the tree tops, and with it all comes a wild and joyous exhilaration. Oh what an experience! Nothing ever equalled it afterwards." The emotions Poague felt during battle were not all simple exhilaration, however. Indeed, he wrote, "I experienced most divers and conflicting emotions – sincere sympathy for individual suffering and wishing I could give relief, and an inner rejoicing and intense satisfaction at the sight of hundreds of my country's foes deliberately put to death."

A battlefield after the action was over was still a terrible place on which to be. John Morton described the scene after the bloody fighting that was Chickamauga: "Everywhere the dying and the dead, the blue and the gray were mixed indiscriminately. The smoke-begrimed, powder-blackened, exhausted Confederates gave to friend and foe alike what assistance they could. The scanty supply of water was given to the wounded and dying, fires were built and the sufferers were brought close to them, and many messages were written by the firelight for the loved ones at home so far away. In one spot a group of the wounded engaged in prayer and singing. In others men raved of wife and home and children, or begged piteously for water."

Wounded artillerymen were taken to brigade hospitals, mostly by members of the Ambulance Corps who were especially picked for the task. These hospitals, in the days before medical personnel were careful about sanitation, were rough affairs, often put in nearby barns, churches, or homes. Inside, doctors cut and hacked away at torn flesh. "The sorriest sights upon a battle-field are in those dreadful field-hospitals, established in barns, under large tents, and in out-houses," William Owen wrote. "The screams and groans of the poor fellows undergoing amputation are sometimes dreadful, – and then the sight of arms and legs surrounding these places, as they are thrown into great piles, is something one that has seen the results of battle can never forget."

In fighting near large cities such as Richmond and Atlanta, wounded men were brought back to central hospitals rather than left in field

The streets of Richmond were filled with wounded after fighting, as here after the Battle of Seven Pines during the Peninsular Campaign.

hospitals. In many cases they were overcrowded, since virtually every Confederate soldier spent some time in a hospital with dysentery or the like during his military career. Those patients who had friends often left to seek aid from them; if they had money, they headed to a hotel, as did Poague, when wounded at the Wilderness. He found the Richmond hospitals overcrowded and caught a cab to the American Hotel where he hired a physician to tend to him. He was also helped by a member of his old battery.

Wounded prisoners also faced danger from their captors, especially if the capturing force were fresh troops or had not seen much action. Private Billy Vaught saw one of his crew members passing through an abandoned Union camp find a wounded Union soldier and "coolly drew his bowie knife & cut the Yankee's throat from ear to ear as he passed him & went on as if he had only snapped a twig."

Other artillerymen took advantage of their richer foes to profit personally. Corporal George Jackson, Jeff Davis Artillery, recalled after one action that one of his crew, "Big Zeke" Melton, "jumped over the breast works and robbed the dead Yankees and brought back fifteen watches and forty or fifty dollars in green backs [legal U.S. currency]." One dead and one wounded Union cavalrymen lay near one of the guns of the Bedford Light Artillery after an attack in April 1865. "Jacob Strasser soon rifled their pockets," recalled Joseph Graves, "and gave the writer a small piece of money as a souvenir." After another battle, John Walters "saw a good pair of boots on a man's feet and as they looked to be about my size, I concluded to appropriate them, to which end I began to pull at them, but while lugging away with a perseverance worthy of a better pair, the leg came off with it just above the knee. As this was more than I bargained for, I left the boots."

Officers still had official duties after the last shot. John Haskell, commanding an artillery battalion at Pickett's Charge, recalled after the artillery had finished and the infantry had gone forward, he "sent out the men able to go, carrying such of the wounded who could move with their help. Then I ordered litters for the wounded who were too badly hurt to get out with only the assistance of their comrades, and had two of the company commanders bring in limber chests and ropes to take out the disabled guns."

At times, however, ill-supplied but victorious Confederates were able to forage after battles. Morton recalled after the battle of Brice's Crossroads: "The men were allowed to forage for themselves among the captured Federal wagons, and they very quickly emptied their haversacks of the cold meat and corn bread they contained. The abundance and variety of the rations provided by 'Uncle Sam' were fairly bewildering to the ever-hungry Confederates. With ham, bacon, coffee, sugar, cheese, and such unusual delicacies to choose from, it is small wonder that the haversacks were filled and refilled as the tempting edibles came to light. The horses, too, munched their rare treats of shelled corn, dry oats, and hay, with evident satisfaction."

Some men were sent officially to hunt on the battlefield after the fighting was finished. Poague, then a lieutenant in a battery, after First Manassas "was sent with a detail to the battle field to gather up the captured guns and harness. In my rounds I came upon many a friend and acquaintance, stiff in death, with whom as boys I had gone to school and college."

One thing many Confederate artillerymen hoped for in battle was to be able to replace old-fashioned 6-pounders, 12-pounder howitzers, or inferior Southern-made guns with superior Northern-made, enemy guns. In fact, this happened a great deal. Morton, whose old battery had two Northern-made 3-inch Ordnance Rifles, often incorrectly called "Rodmans", recalled that his men "had been hoping ever since the capture of two guns of this superior make at Lexington to secure a complete battery of Rodman's rifle guns. With a shout of wild triumph, the artillerymen of this battery, without waiting for orders, bore down upon the captured pieces and quickly exchanged them with the two 12-pound brass howitzers, which were still warm from action, and turned the newly acquired pieces upon the now fleeing enemy." Battery commander Chamberlayne reported after Chancellorsville that "pulled off 2 captured rifles, since that I have exchanged my Nap[oleo]ns for Parrotes [Parrotts] & now have a complete 4 gun Battery of Rifle Guns." The Rockbridge Artillery replaced its Southern-made inferior quality guns with two 20-pounder Parrotts captured at Harper's Ferry, a 12-pounder Napoleon captured in front of Richmond, and two 20-pounder Parrotts captured at Winchester in June, 1863.

Confederate prisoners at Camp Douglas, near Chicago, a mixture of artillerymen and troops from other branches. Life was so bad at times there that the place was known as the "Andersonville of the North", after the infamous Southern prison camp that had a very high mortality rate. (Frank Leslie's Illustrated News)

COLOR PLATE COMMENTARY

A: CORPORAL, 3D COMPANY, RICHMOND HOWITZERS, WITH ISSUE EQUIPMENT
(1) The gunner's haversack was used to carry a live round from the limber chest, where the fuse was set, to the gun for loading. (2) The gunner's pouch was worn on a brown leather belt with a plain iron roller buckle and was used to carry friction primers (2a). The lanyard (3) was used to fire the weapon. There was only one official issue artilleryman's weapon, a sword. The longer sword with the curved blade (4) is a light artilleryman's saber, a Southern-made copy of a U.S. Army weapon that was actually useless and usually abandoned along a line of march to be picked up by Quartermaster troops who turned them over to the cavalry. This particular model was made by a Southern manufacturer who, lacking enough iron for scabbards, used brass instead. The short sword (5), a copy of a French copy of the Roman sword, was issued to foot artillery with the idea they could use it against horses in an attack. In fact, if any weapon was carried, it was some type of revolver, such as the Leech & Rigdon Southern-made version of the Colt 0.36 caliber Navy revolver (6).

B: ROCKBRIDGE ARTILLERY ON THE MARCH
Mud was the bane of the artilleryman's existence. Since the horses alone could not pull the combination of caisson, limber, and gun on deeply rutted muddy roads, it was up to the cannoneers to help. The uniforms shown here are based on original descriptions of members of the famed Virginia Rockbridge Artillery. John Walters, Norfolk Light Artillery Blues, recalled one road that was so muddy that the cannoneers were "compelled to take all the horses off one piece and hitch them to another and drawing it a mile or so return and get another, till all were once more together."

C: THE CRENSHAW BATTERY MOVES UP A PIECE BY HAND
The drill for moving a piece forward by hand, done at the front with the horses safely in the rear, called for four men pulling on the limber, while four men pushed the gun up from the rear. The lieutenant supervising the drill wears a prewar Virginia dark blue frock coat with U.S. Army officer's insignia on each shoulder. Behind them are men of New Orleans' famed Washington Artillery Battalion stationed along the James River in 1862. The men came from Louisiana in their prewar dark blue uniforms.

D: A CONFEDERATE GUN CREW ATTEMPTS TO REMOVE A 12-POUNDER NAPOLEON BY PROLONGUE
Union troops attack Confederate positions on the left of Missionary Ridge as the cannoneers attempt to remove their piece by prolongue. The Union troops came up the steep ridge so quickly, emerging suddenly right on top of the Confederate line, that no defense was possible. Artillery was especially defenseless since the men could not depress their guns enough to fire on Union troops climbing the heights. They had been positioned to fire into the city of Chattanooga, far to their front. Note that all of them wear jackets as made in Georgia depots, with branch-of-service color cuffs and collar, but few have artillery red. It was noted that most artillerymen in the Army of Tennessee wore infantry blue collars and cuffs instead of red ones.

E: THE LOUISIANA GUARD ARTILLERY DEFENDS KELLY'S FORD
On November 7, ·1864, the Louisiana Guard Artillery, supported by infantry from Rodes' Division, was holding a position covering Kelly's Ford across the Rappahannock. Overwhelming numbers of Union infantry stormed across the river, forcing the battery to lose its four guns along with 41 officers and enlisted men. The preferred way of deploying a section or battery was *en échelon*. At this range they would fire solid shot, switching to shell and eventually to canister as the enemy approaches.

F: ALLEGHENY ARTILLERY FIRING
This four-gun battery is in different stages of the loading operation. When the firing procedure began, according to Andrews' manual, "The gunner is at the end of the trail handspike; **No. 1** and **No. 2** are about *two* feet outside the wheels, No. 1 on the right, and No. 2 on the left; with howitzers, rather in rear of the muzzle; with guns, in line with the front part of the wheels; **No. 3** and **No. 4** are in line with the knob of the cascabel, covering No. 1 and 2; **No. 5** is *five* yards in rear of the left wheel; **No. 6** in rear of the limber, and **No. 7** on his left, covering No. 5; **No. 8**, the chief of the caisson, is *four* yards in rear of the limber, and on its left; all face to the front.

"The chief of the piece [labeled **CP**] is opposite the middle of the trail handspike, outside and near the left cannoneers. In actual firing he takes his place on the right or left, where he can best observe the effect of the shot."

Loading (A) When ready to fire, the chief of the piece commanded, "Load by detail, Load," followed by a pause, then slowly enough for the men to act, the numbers, "two, three, four."

On command "Load" No. 1 faced left, stepping obliquely to the right with the right foot· without moving his left and, at the same time, brought the sponge smartly to a perpendicular position by drawing his right hand up in line with the elbow. No. 2 faced to the right and took an oblique step to the left corresponding to the movements of No. 1. No. 3 stepped to the left, wiped the vent-field with a leather thumbstall, which he then held pressed on the vent, keeping his elbow raised; his fingers on the left side of the piece so as to allow the gunner to point over his thumb; the right hand on the tube-pouch. No. 4 inserted the lanyard hook into the ring of a primer and stood fast. No. 5 ran to the ammunition chest, posted 11 yards in the rear of the piece, and received from No. 7 or No. 6 a single round. He took the shot in his right hand and the cartridge in his left, placed it in a leather haversack especially designed for the purpose, and brought it back to No. 2. He then returned immediately for another round, halting at his place until the piece was fired. When the ammunition called for was shell or spherical case, No. 5 had to show the fuze to the gunner, who checked it was cut to the right time, before delivering the charge to No. 2.

On the command "Two" No. 1 stepped oblique to the left with his left foot, planting it about half way between the piece and the wheel, and opposite the muzzle. He brought the sponge across his body to the left, holding the sponge staff about a 45° angle. No. 2 placed himself near the muzzle of the piece.

On hearing "Three" No. 1 took a side step about 30 inches to the right and, bending his right knee, brought the sponge to a horizontal position with the sponge-head against the face of the muzzle. No. 2 brought his left foot to the side of the right and faced to the right, bringing his hands together to receive the ammunition from No. 5. The cartridge went into the right hand and the shot in the left.

On "Four" No. 1 dropped his left hand behind his thigh, straightened his right knee and, bending over the left, slammed the sponge home.

"Sponge!" was the next command.

At this command, No. 1 glanced over to see that No. 3 had his thumbstall clearly closing the vent to prevent air getting into the tube. Then he gave two turns to the sponge, being careful to press it hard against the end of the bore, all the time keeping his eye on the vent rather than the muzzle. On the second motion, No. 1 withdrew the sponge, straightening his left knee and bending his right. He grabbed the staff near the sponge-head with his left hand, back of the hand down, and placed the sponge against the face of the piece. On the third motion he turned the sponge, bringing the staff horizontal and extending the hands to the ends of the staff. In really heated action, cannoneers would eliminate sponging as a step; indeed, there was some thinking that this was safer anyway.

The sponge withdrawn, No. 2 faced to his right and placed the ammunition into the muzzle, taking care that the seam on the cloth cartridge did not come under the vent, and then stepped back, left foot first, to his post outside the wheel. Then he faced No. 1, both feet together in the position of attention. On the command "Ready!" he then waited, left leg straight and right leg bent, and his eye on the muzzle throughout the firing process.

Once the charge was in the muzzle, No. 1 placed his rammer head into the muzzle, shoving the charge in only slightly.

At the same time, No. 3 moved to the end of the trail handspike. Grabbing it with both hands, he got ready to move it to the right or left on a signal of the gunner. The gunner came up to the rear of the piece and aimed it, tapping the right of the trail to signal No. 3 to move to the left, or the left of the trail to move to the right. Once the gunner was satisfied with the aim, he raised both hands and No. 3 returned to his original position as the gunner returned to his.

"Ram!" came the next command. No. 1 then rammed the charge home, throwing the weight of his body on to the rammer, bending his left knee and passing his left arm, the elbow slightly bent and back of the hand up, in a horizontal position until it pointed in the direction of the left trunnion. His right shoulder was thrown back and his eyes faced the front until he felt the cartridge was firmly seated home.

Then he jerked the sponge out with the right hand, and straightened his body to the position of attention. Holding the sponge close to the body, on the next motion he stepped back outside the wheel, ending up with the rammer head resting on his right toe.

Pricking the cartridge (B) "Ready!" was the next command. At this, No. 2, as mentioned, bent into the firing

position, as did No. 1, who also dropped the end of the sponge staff into his left hand. No. 3 pulled his vent pick out, stepped to the vent and pricked the flannel cartridge bag. He had to take care here not to move the cartridge forward in doing this. No. 4 stepped with his right foot to the vent, dropped the friction primer tube into the vent, and took the lanyard in his right hand. He then moved to the rear, beyond the rear of the piece, until the lanyard was still slack but could be stretched. Then No. 3 covered the vent with his left hand as soon as the primer was inserted.

Firing (C and D) "Fire!" was the final command. On hearing it, No. 3 quickly stepped clear of the wheel. As soon as No. 4 saw him in his proper place, he pulled the lanyard briskly and firmly in a downward direction to the rear so as to keep the lanyard hook from flying back into his face. If the weapon successfully fired, everyone returned to their original positions to prepare for the next shot.

If the primer failed, the gunner immediately called out, "Don't advance, the primer has failed." On this command, No. 2 stepped inside the wheel, close to the axletree. No. 3 passed a priming wire over the wheel to him while No. 4 gave him another primer. No. 2 then pricked the cartridge again, inserted the new friction primer, and stepped back to his firing position. The command "Fire!" was given again. In most cases, this proved the charm. If not, the process was repeated until the section chief decided there was a serious flaw in something and had the gun withdrawn to be worked on and put back into firing order.

G: SEACOAST FORT GUNS

Coastal forts used large guns that were manned by the heavy artillery. Two types of gun are shown in this composite illustration. The British-made Armstrong gun (A) is a 150-pounder muzzle loading rifle, mounted on a barbette carriage. It was the pride of the South's last major seacoast fort, Fort Fisher, North Carolina, whose fall in early 1864 marked the end of the South's ability to import munitions and civilian goods. The fort was manned by members of the 36th Regiment North Carolina Troops (2d Regiment North Carolina Artillery). Its men largely wore plain gray jeans-cloth uniforms made in a North Carolina quartermaster depot. Also shown are men loading a shell into a 12.75-inch British-made Blakely rifle (B), with the unique loading hoist on the top of its muzzle. These huge guns protected Southern ports from Federal naval attacks for most of the war.

H: QUARTERS IN THE FIELD

Shelter halves were often acquired from Union army sources, and were shared by two cannoneers: those without would make their beds under the sky. Confederate soldiers were noted for preferring to camp in the woods, rather than the open fields as did Union soldiers. One of the hardest things Confederate artillerymen had to do on campaign was to keep clean. Usually an individual in every battery served as a barber, shaving his partners whenever they had the chance. Note the African-Americans, two of thousands who accompanied the army as cooks, foragers, musicians, and all-around servants. One soldier reads a letter to his illiterate companion as they await their turn for a shave.

I: A BATTALION WINTER HEADQUARTERS

In the winter, log huts were built by all the men, with one larger building used as a battalion headquarters. The bunks were used by the adjutant and quartermaster, while the field-grade officers each had individual huts. The building made an office during the day and a social headquarters in the evening. Women, as seen here, often visited their husbands when in winter quarters and made evenings brighter. As well, African-American slaves, usually wearing issue Confederate uniforms which often confused Northern observers into thinking they were regular enlisted fighting men, waited on them.

J: THE PERSONAL ITEMS OF AN ARTILLERYMAN

The artilleryman needed a number of items to make life in the field acceptable. The government issued a haversack (1), most of which were made of simple white cotton, in which to carry rations, often only an ear or two of Indian corn, and mess items such as a tin cup and plate: an alternative type is also shown (1a). A canteen to carry water was supplied and since metal was in demand for weapons, most Southern-made canteens were made of wood. Shown are two such canteens, a Nichols pattern version (2) made out of two hollowed out pieces of wood and nailed together, and a Gardiner pattern version (3), made like a small cask with a hole on top. These holes had tops, but they were made of thin wood that generally broke under use and most of them after a short time were topless, as shown here. Southern soldiers generally had tobacco available (4) and a pipe (5), if rations were in short supply, and they carried it in a small pouch sometimes suspended from a jacket button (6). Every man needed a sewing kit, or "housewife" (7) as it was called, a toothbrush (8), and a comb (9). Generally each man had several small bags (10) for such items as salt when available. Also shown is a typical soldier's wallet of the period (11).

BIBLIOGRAPHY

Andrews, R. Snowden, *Andrews' Mounted Artillery Drill*, Charleston, South Carolina, 1863

Bergeron, Jr., Arthur W., and Hewitt, Lawrence L., *Boone's Louisiana Battery*, Baton Rouge, Louisiana, 1986

Chamberlayne, C.G., *Ham Chamberlayne – Virginian, Letters and Papers of an Artillery Officer*, Wilmington, North Carolina, 1992

Cockrell, Monroe F., ed., *Gunner With Stonewall*, Wilmington, North Carolina, 1987

Haskell, John, *The Haskell Memoirs*, New York, New York, 1960

Daniel, Larry J., *Cannoneers in Gray, The Field Artillery of the Army of Tennessee, 1861–1865*, University, Alabama, 1984

Douglas, Lucia R., *Douglas' Texas Battery, CSA*, Tyler, Texas, 1966

Gilham, William, *Manual of Instruction of the Volunteers and Militia of the United States*, Philadelphia, Pennsylvania, 1861

Graves, Joseph A., *The History of the Bedford Light Artillery, 1861–1865*, Bedford City, Virginia, 1903

Hughes, Jr., Nathaniel C., *The Civil War Memoir of Philip Daingerfield Stephenson, D.D.*, Conway, Arkansas, 1995

Hughes, Jr., Nathaniel C., *The Pride of the Confederate Artillery, The Washington Artillery in the Army of Tennessee*, Baton Rouge, Louisiana, 1997

Laboda, Lawrence R., *From Selma to Appomattox, The History of the Jeff Davis Artillery*, New York, New York, 1994

McCarthy, Carlton, *Detailed Minutiae of Soldier Life*, Richmond, Virginia, 1882

Moore, Edward A., *The Story of a Cannoneer Under Stonewall Jackson*, Washington, DC, 1907

Morton, Capt. John W., *The Artillery of Nathan Bedford Forrest's Cavalry*, Marietta, Georgia, 1995

Owen, William M., *In Camp And Battle with the Washington Artillery*, Boston, Massachusetts, 1885

Stiles, Robert, *Four Years Under Marse Robert*, Dayton, Ohio, 1988

Welker, David, ed. *A Keystone Rebel, The Civil War Diary of Joseph Garey, Hudson's Battery, Mississippi Volunteers*, Gettysburg, Pennsylvania, 1996

Wiley, Ken, *Norfolk Blues, The Civil War Diary of the Norfolk Light Artillery Blues*, Shippensburg, Pennsylvania, 1997

INDEX

Figures in **bold** refer to illustrations